Learning in the Face of Adversity

A WORLD BANK STUDY

Learning in the Face of Adversity

*The UNRWA Education Program
for Palestine Refugees*

Husein Abdul-Hamid, Harry Anthony Patrinos, Joel Reyes,
Jo Kelcey, and Andrea Diaz Varela

WORLD BANK GROUP

Contents

Boxes

Figures

Tables

Preface

Since 2009, as part of the World Bank–supported Middle East and North Africa Regional Network for Education Research, the Palestinian Authority Ministry of Education (covering the West Bank and Gaza) has been examining learning outcomes at United Nations Relief and Works Agency (UNRWA) schools. It found that in 2007 UNRWA students outperformed students attending public schools by more than a year's worth of learning in the International Association for the Evaluation of Educational Achievement's Trends in International Mathematics and Science Study (TIMSS) assessment. This was also found to be true in Jordan. In 2011, both the UNRWA and public systems reflected declines in TIMSS scores; UNRWA schools still showed a significant student performance advantage. Given the resource-constrained administration and the various sources of adversity facing students and teachers—especially refugees, who often suffer disproportionate physical, emotional, and psychological disadvantages—the findings raise questions about what lies behind such results.

This mixed methods research study was undertaken to better understand the reasons for success at UNRWA schools and their positive variation from comparable public schools. Econometric techniques were used to analyze international (TIMSS and Programme for International Student Assessment [PISA]) and national learning achievement data. Pedagogical practices and classroom time-on-task were observed using structured methods (Stallings model). Systems Approach for Better Education Results (SABER) tools were used to better understand the policies and implementation strategies for school and teacher management and for monitoring and evaluation. Additionally, qualitative data were collected and analyzed in line with an education resilience conceptual framework to better uncover factors that help students develop the skills to learn despite the adversities they face.

The goal of this study is to allow us to better understand how a school system can operate efficiently under adversity. The results of this work will be useful in identifying relevant policies in the region. These findings will also be shared with other countries in conflict or postconflict situations to share findings on how schools can remain effective and relevant and perform well in difficult contexts.

Our community is interested in and appreciates learning. The school ensures the students like going there and enjoy the learning that happens. The goal of the school is to create well-educated students. My family also has a big role in learning, and they will be happy when I finish my learning and graduate from the university with high grades.

Female student, Gaza

Foreword

The Systems Approach for Better Education Results (SABER) initiative is designed to help countries identify actionable priorities for strengthening education systems so that all children and youth can be equipped with knowledge and skills for life. Any education system is a complex network of providers and beneficiaries, institutions, and individuals whose efforts and interactions determine whether the country is using resources effectively to advance learning for all.

While building schools, equipping classrooms, and providing textbooks are all important, merely increasing inputs is not enough to improve student learning. Evidence shows that how schools and school systems use those resources matters a great deal in driving learning. At the World Bank, we focus on improving the non-input factors that drive learning—the information flow, accountability relationships, incentives, financing structures, and behaviors, especially the presence and actions of good teachers to ensure learning.

This book applies the systems approach to explain how a school system responsible for helping educate refugees is achieving relatively high results. There is much to learn from the United Nations Relief and Works Agency (UNRWA) schools for Palestine refugees. This book highlights the fact that in a context of adversity and conflict, an education system requires more than the mainstream education model. It demands also a resilience approach. From the mainstream lens, the UNRWA system exhibits the effective classroom practices of teachers, strong school leadership, assessments, and shared accountability for learning, which support organizational adaptability and performance in the face of adversity. A resilience approach also calls for the recognition of the risks and vulnerabilities that students face and a commitment to foster relevant interactions across school and community actors towards the protection, well-being and learning of students in such challenging contexts. A resilience approach does not imply that schools and communities at risk are left to fend alone, but calls for an alignment and institutionalization of relevant education services and systems to foster and support the resilience processes of which students, teachers, and families avail themselves.

The UNRWA experience provides insights into systems-level efforts that sustain, amidst a difficult context, quality learning opportunities for all children and youth. Any system can draw lessons from this experience by building on the model to create a community and culture of learning. It must recognize the adversity of vulnerable groups and promote collaboration among the school, the teacher, the parent, and the community, all focusing on student achievement, protection, and well-being. School systems need to gauge and promote a set of assets and opportunities that better support students to manage the adversities they face, protecting them from harm, and helping them achieve their educational outcomes. Even in rapidly changing contexts, assessing these assets and opportunities is crucial to understanding why educational outcomes are achieved and how to support such processes.

Certainly this is a book that shows that even under very difficult situations, quality education is possible and the experience of the UNRWA schools provides great lessons for school systems that face similar challenges.

Claudia Maria Costin
Senior Director
Education Global Practice
World Bank Group
Washington, DC

Acknowledgments

Many individuals have provided valuable inputs and suggestions for this work. Particular thanks are due to the peer reviewers: Raja Bentaouet-Kattan, Tazeen Fasih, and Suhas Parandekar. Mourad Ezzine, Ernesto Cuadra, Elizabeth King, and Robin Horn provided support. Emilio Porta was instrumental in setting the groundwork for this study by collecting important in-country data, Emily Brearley provided support in the literature review, and Shaista Baksh provided the logistics support for the study. Special thanks to Halsey Rogers for his comments and feedback on the analysis and the write-up.

Special thanks are also due to the staff and students of the UNRWA Education Program in the West Bank and Gaza and Jordan, as well the public education systems of the Palestinian Authority and the Hashemite Kingdom of Jordan, who greatly facilitated the implementation of this research. This study would not have been possible without the support of the local field data collection team. Students, teachers, and school principals graciously allowed us into their classrooms and provided valuable insights into their often-difficult lives and education experiences. A significant part of this work was possible only because of their willingness to share important insights and feedback about what helped them learn.

Special thanks to Veronica Grigera, Sarah Mintz, Namrata Saraogi, Jessica Cross, Nicky Corbett, and Cassia Miranda for reviewing and editing the final document.

This work was made possible by the Rapid Social Response Program, supported by Norway, the Russian Federation, and the UK Department for International Development (DfID), and the DfID–World Bank Partnership for Education Development.

Executive Summary: The UNRWA Story

Palestine refugees are achieving higher-than-average learning outcomes in spite of the adverse circumstances they live under. Their education system—the United Nations Relief and Works Agency (UNRWA) for Palestine refugees in the Near East—operates one of the largest nongovernmental school systems in the Middle East. It manages nearly 700 schools, has hired 17,000 staff, educates more than 500,000 refugee students each year, and operates in five areas, including the West Bank and Gaza, Jordan, Lebanon, and the Syrian Arab Republic. Contrary to what might be expected from a resource-constrained administration serving refugee students who continually face a multitude of adversities, UNRWA students outperform public schools in the three regions—the West Bank and Gaza and Jordan—by a year's worth of learning.

This study uses a mixed methods research approach,[1] incorporating both quantitative and qualitative research to address the complexity of the research question and its exploratory nature, namely, *How do UNRWA schools continually and consistently outperform public schools?* This study was prepared using the following tools, techniques, and data collection:

- Econometric techniques were used to analyze learning achievement data, including international (Trends in International Mathematics and Science Study [TIMSS] and Programme for International Student Assessment [PISA]) and national student assessment data.
- The Systems Approach for Better Education Results (SABER) tools and rubrics were used to assess different system components, such as teacher effectiveness, school autonomy, and student assessments.
- Stallings classroom observations provided a structured method to compare teachers' and students' interactions.
- Qualitative data collected through interviews captured the lived experiences of a sample of UNRWA students.

These tools were applied through a concurrent research process (see figure ES.1), constituted through a mixed methods research design that led to integrated findings.

Figure ES.1 Sequential Mixed Methods Methodology Design

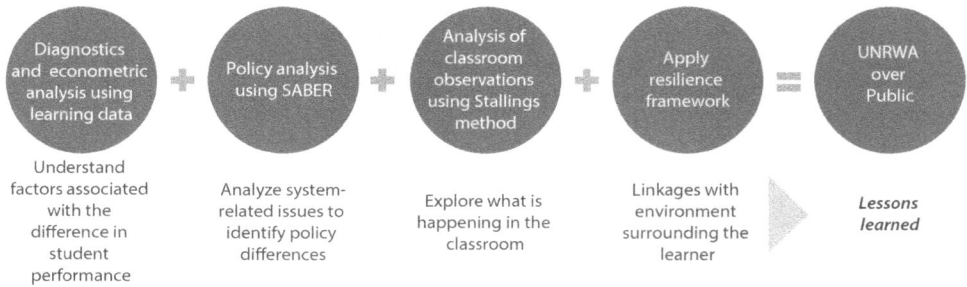

| Diagnostics and econometric analysis using learning data | + | Policy analysis using SABER | + | Analysis of classroom observations using Stallings method | + | Apply resilience framework | = | UNRWA over Public |

Understand factors associated with the difference in student performance   Analyze system-related issues to identify policy differences   Explore what is happening in the classroom   Linkages with environment surrounding the learner   *Lessons learned*

Note: UNRWA = United Nations Relief and Works Agency.

It is important to recognize the methodological and practical limitations of this study to establish its relevance to other education systems and contexts of adversity. The UNRWA system covers five regions, of which this study examines three: the West Bank and Gaza and Jordan. Thus, the findings represent factors that appear to be working within a system, but they do not imply that the system as a whole is achieving positive results. That would require additional data collection and analysis for Lebanon and the Syrian Arab Republic. Nor do the findings attempt to negate or discount the incidence of falling standards in UNRWA schools in recent years. Moreover, the international assessment data point to UNRWA's performance in relation to the public system in some of the host countries. But the data do not cover the inputs and processes in public school systems, which may differ from those in UNRWA schools, so they cannot be used to pass judgment on what these public systems may face. Although the focus of this report is on the assets that have added value to learning in UNRWA, a more comprehensive review of the UNRWA system may consider other related studies.

International assessment data from 2007 were analyzed to assess learning outcomes of these schools, and the explanatory data, to which the bulk of this study is dedicated, were collected in 2011. Results of 2011 test scores, however, demonstrated a decrease in learning outcomes for both the public sector and UNRWA schools. Although overall standards have decreased, a controlled analysis of these results adjusted for the same range of variables as the 2007 results still illustrates UNRWA's learning outcomes to be significantly higher for the West Bank and Gaza and Jordan. This situation aligns to our understanding of resilience not as an outcome in itself but as a process in contexts of adversity. Both the 2007 and 2011 data suggest that the UNRWA system is gauging and promoting a set of assets and opportunities that better support its students in "navigating" the adversities they face. Even in rapidly changing contexts, and with concomitant results, assessing these assets and opportunities is crucial to understanding why outcomes are achieved and how to support such processes.

Main Takeaways from the Research

UNRWA Schools Continually and Consistently Outperform Public Schools by a Margin Equivalent to More than One Additional Year of Learning.

This is achieved as a result of the way these schools recruit, prepare, and support teachers; because of instructional practices and pedagogy in the classroom; and because of school leadership, accountability, and mutual support. This has created a distinguished learning community centered on the student. Of note:

- UNRWA selects, prepares, and supports its education staff to pursue high learning outcomes.
- Time-on-task is high in UNRWA schools, and this time is used more effectively than in public schools.
- UNRWA schools have a world-class assessment and accountability system.
- UNRWA schools are part of a wider community and culture of learning that supports the child and ensures that the education received is meaningful and relevant.

UNRWA Schools Increase Student Performance

Analysis points to significantly higher scores in relation to the mastery of curriculum content and cognitive learning domains. Moreover, more UNRWA students achieve the international benchmarks in math and science. On average, UNRWA students in Jordan and the West Bank and Gaza achieve scores 23–80 points higher than their peers at public schools, even after controlling for student characteristics and for urban or rural contexts.

Performance of UNRWA Students Is Higher than Their Peers despite Two Important Parental and Teacher Characteristics.

One would expect that socioeconomic status or parental education would be highly associated with performance, as documented in the education literature. But UNRWA students outperform their peers in public schools despite their socioeconomic disadvantages. Differentiating factors include student self-confidence, as well as parental support and involvement in school activities. Figure ES.2 shows how increased parental involvement and support leads to improved student performance.

One would also expect that teachers' academic qualifications would be associated with student performance, but this is not the case. Students at UNRWA schools outperformed students at public schools despite having teachers with the same years of service and degrees completed as their counterparts in public schools. The most important factors in explaining this performance gap were teachers' confidence in teaching the subject matter, job satisfaction, and ongoing professional development and training. At UNRWA schools, 75 percent of teachers are either satisfied or highly satisfied with their jobs, compared with roughly 50 percent in public schools (figure ES.3).

Figure ES.2   Parents Are More Involved in UNRWA Schools

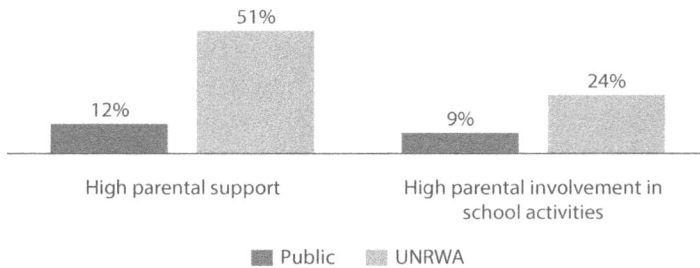

Source: TIMSS Study 2007 data.
Note: UNRWA = United Nations Relief and Works Agency.

Figure ES.3   Teachers at UNRWA Schools Are More Satisfied with Their Jobs

percentage satisfied or highly satisfied

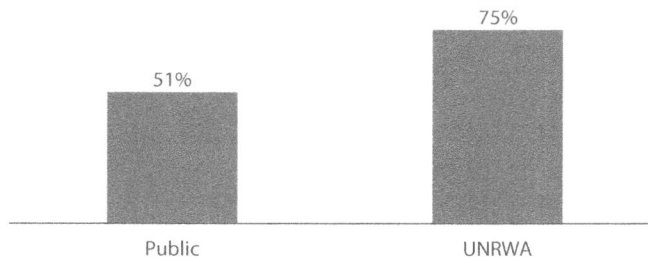

Source: TIMSS Study 2007 data.
Note: UNRWA = United Nations Relief and Works Agency.

From the perspective of UNRWA students, teachers demonstrate their satis-faction and pedagogical confidence through their interaction with students inside and outside of the classroom. This is epitomized by the responses of two students in Gaza who, when asked what helps them to learn, responded:

> The teacher, the teacher is a role model. He is teaching us the right things and does so in an excellent way, using worksheets, media, and group work.

> > Male student, Gaza

> Teachers always support me and make me participate in Ecompetitions such as math competitions in Gaza and Khan-Younis. And my English teacher always asks me to write essays in English because she wants to motivate me. I also always get rewards from school, which encourages me to work harder and to study harder: When you love your teacher, you always try your best to get high marks in her class.

> > Female student, Gaza

Figure ES.4 Advantage in Test Scores for UNRWA over Public Schools, Controlling for Stated Factors

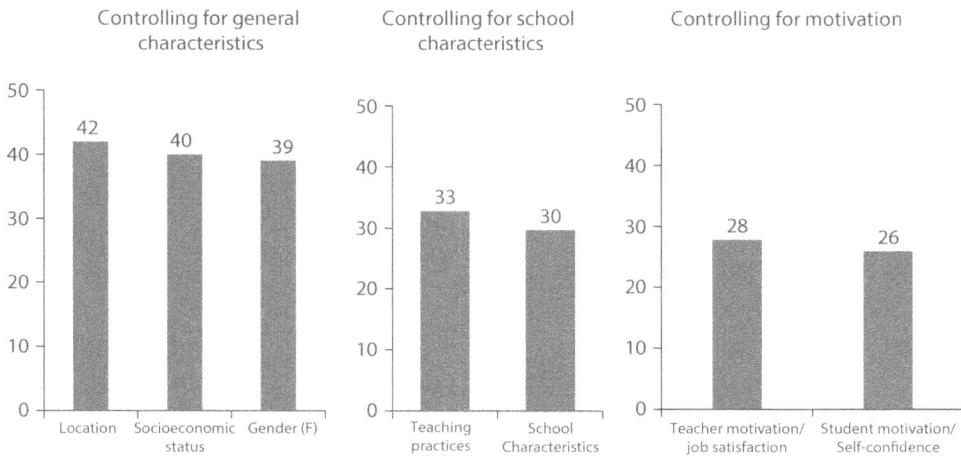

Sources: TIMSS 2007.

The UNRWA advantage in learning outcomes—despite apparent commonalities with public schools—is 25 points, a quarter of a standard deviation, or about a year's worth of learning. Once other factors are controlled for, the differential declines but remains at 26 points, which is equivalent to a full year of learning (as shown in figure ES.4). Understanding those not easily observable factors that may account for the noted learning scores differences is the focus of this study.

These higher learning outcomes are achieved teaching the same curriculum as the public schools in their host countries, at a lower unit cost and with unstable funding that could decline from one year to the next. The cost per student in UNRWA schools is 20 percent less than in public schools in Jordan. (figure ES.5 demonstrates that the cost per student in UNRWA schools is much less as compared with public schools.)

UNRWA Schools Provide Critical Support for Teachers and Management
UNRWA schools use the curriculum of the host authority in a given field of operation. Therefore, teachers and associated school management structures, as the main mechanism for implementing the curriculum, can provide a source of variation to understand differences in learning outcomes. Based on this, we analyzed data on selection, preparation, and support of teachers as key learning support attributes of the UNRWA system.

UNRWA Is More Successful at Attracting and Recruiting High-Quality Teachers
UNRWA teachers' colleges attract the best high school graduates to enroll free of charge and with guaranteed employment after completion and upon meeting

Figure ES.5   Cost per Student in Jordan's UNRWA Schools and Public Schools

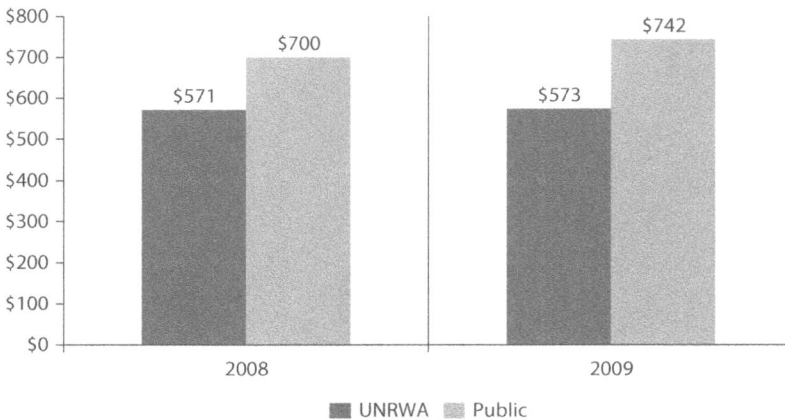

Sources: Public expenditure review and UNRWA annual financial reports 2008 and 2009.
Note: UNRWA = United Nations Relief and Works Agency.

the high standards set. Before recruitment, UNRWA teachers are also interviewed and are required to pass a written exam. As a result, the UNRWA system appears to have created a sound built-in quality control that is lacking in the public system.

Clear Expectations Are Set for UNRWA Teachers, Who Receive Guidance and Mentoring Services

UNRWA teachers are provided with explicit standards regarding what students must know and be able to do, and they receive direction on how to achieve these standards. Teachers also benefit from guidance on how to effectively use their time in the classroom, and there is a clear and official focus on time on task. Teachers additionally support the development and implementation of school plans, design curricular material, and take part in the evaluation of activities.

UNRWA Has More Mandated Ongoing Professional Development and Orientation for Teachers than Public Schools

Although both public and UNRWA school systems require at least four years of college education to become a primary school teacher, UNRWA also requires classroom experience (built into the curriculum at their teachers' colleges). In addition, all new teachers must complete a mandatory two-year intensive and structured training program focused on classroom instruction after they are hired.

Teachers at UNRWA Schools Are Supported by Well-Qualified, Well-Prepared, and Experienced School Principals

The UNRWA system invests heavily in preparing and developing qualified school principals through programs designed to support school-based leadership through coursework and mentoring. School principals are required to evaluate teacher performance and provide guidance for curriculum and teaching-related tasks. Student narratives point to a keen awareness of their principal's abilities. A female student in Gaza spoke of her principal in this way:

> When we have difficulty understanding a teacher, she listens to us and talks to the teacher. She tries her best to solve the problem. She also maintains peace at school. She provides the atmosphere necessary for us to learn. She urges teachers to come to school early to give reinforcement classes. She also urges students to be kind to each other and help each other ... in addition to giving us advice about how to prepare for exams.

> Female student, Gaza

The UNRWA System Has Fewer Management Layers and Is More Accountable for Student Outcomes than Public Schools

UNRWA and public schools are similar in many aspects; both have limited autonomy with regard to budget, financing, and personnel. But they differ significantly in terms of assessment and accountability: UNRWA has a world class assessment system and is more accountable than the public schools (as shown in table ES.1).

UNRWA has established a well-defined and carefully implemented accountability system to assess and support teaching and learning. Assessments are a priority and are disseminated to teachers (to inform lesson plans and instructional practices) and to policy makers. Teachers are also required to participate in internal and external monitoring and evaluation. Whereas both public and UNRWA evaluation systems include classroom observations and multiple criteria, UNRWA evaluations are more rigorous and frequent. Professional development and performance evaluations are requirements to remain in the teaching

Table ES.1 Comparison between UNRWA and Public Systems Policies in School Management and Autonomy

Dimension	Public Jordan	UNRWA	Public Palestine
Budget autonomy	●○○○	●○○○	●○○○
Personnel autonomy	●●○○	●●○○	●●○○
Participation finance	●○○○	●○○○	●○○○
Assessment	●●○○	●●●●	●●○○
Accountability	●●○○	●●●○	●●○○

Source: World Bank 2011.
Note: ●○○○ = latent, ●●○○ = emerging, ●●●○ = established, ●●●● = mature or best practice. UNRWA = United Nations Relief and Works Agency.

profession within the UNRWA system, with incentives for good performance and sanctions for poor performance. Although accountability assessments point to an established system within UNRWA, more formal school-based structures for community participation in this process could help UNRWA achieve a more mature accountability system at the school level. Existing positive relations between families, communities, and teaching staff provide the foundation for this (see the final summation on community and culture of learning).

UNRWA Schools Promote High-Quality Teaching and Classroom Time

UNRWA teachers, in addition to being well prepared and supported, operate differently in the classroom than those in the public system. The proportion of time spent on learning activities in UNRWA schools compares favorably with successful systems in developed countries. UNRWA schools appear to use this time to engage students through confidently led collaborative activities, discussions, and assignments, all promoting greater student participation.

There Is Less Wasted Time in UNRWA Schools

Quality teaching and instruction are the main focuses at UNRWA schools. In Jordan, 90 percent of teachers' working time is dedicated to teaching, compared with less than 60 percent at public schools. Teachers in UNRWA schools are also supported by mentors to improve their instructional capacities. There are fewer incidences of students being off-task in UNRWA classrooms as a result.

Teacher Practices at UNRWA Schools Reflect a High Level of Confidence to Teach Various Subjects through a Variety of Methods.

Teachers in UNRWA schools seem to have confidence to engage with multiple approaches rather than a single pedagogical tool. They facilitate learning through innovative techniques supported by multiple classroom materials and teaching aids. Illustrative materials relevant to subject content are also posted in classrooms.

Teachers in UNRWA Schools Implement More Interactive Learning Activities, Discussions, and Assignments

UNRWA classrooms provide greater opportunities for discussions and debates, as well as for asking questions than in public schools (figure ES.6). There are more cooperative activities on projects and group work. Students are more engaged working on assignments and classwork such as solving problems. The focus is on interaction and problem solving, rather than on lecturing, as at public schools.

Students in UNRWA Classrooms Participate at Higher Levels than in Public Schools through Structured Activities

Students in UNRWA schools spend more time taking notes and collaborating on learning activities. In this way, they are able to interact further with the subject material and may be more encouraged to synthesize, analyze, and prioritize. They

Figure ES.6   More Interaction and Less Lecturing in UNRWA Schools

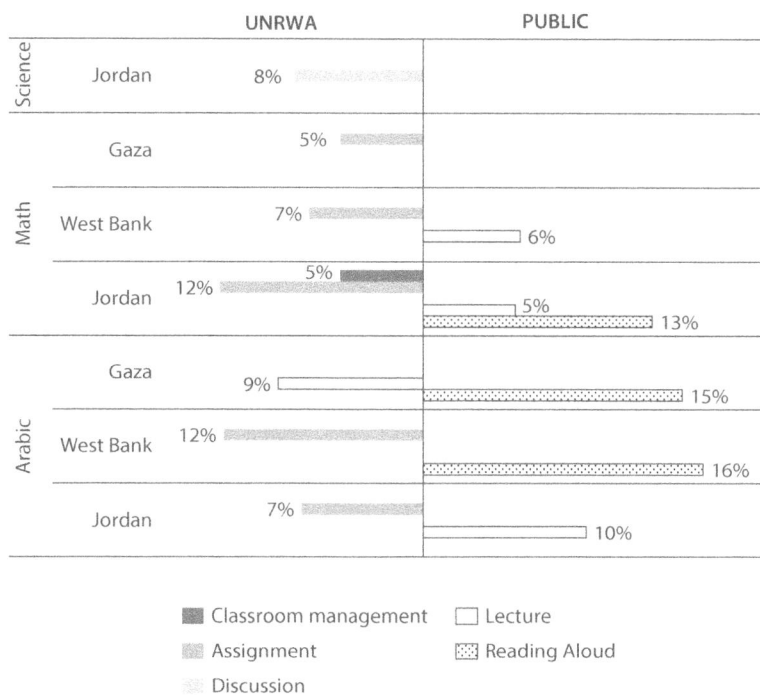

		UNRWA	PUBLIC
Science	Jordan	8%	
	Gaza	5%	
Math	West Bank	7%	6%
	Jordan	12% / 5%	5% / 13%
Arabic	Gaza	9%	15%
	West Bank	12%	16%
	Jordan	7%	10%

■ Classroom management   ☐ Lecture

░ Assignment   ▓ Reading Aloud

░ Discussion

Source: World Bank classroom observations 2011.
Note: UNRWA = United Nations Relief and Works Agency.

are also able to interact more with each other. Indeed, peer academic support was an important theme in the student narratives. As one explained:

> Teaching is excellent; they give information in a good way to the students and nothing is left out of our learning. They ask us if there is any need to explain things again. The teachers make peer groups and each group has an excellent student in it who teaches the others. I was in one of these groups and had four students with me.
>
> Male student, Gaza

One incentive for collaborative learning may be that graded activities assessed by the teacher are more common in UNRWA schools. Students in UNRWA schools are not only engaged in a variety of functions during class, but the percentage of classes in which students work on graded activities is higher. Student work is assessed, and feedback expected. Quizzes and exams are common, and teachers are more likely to review material when preparing for a test in UNRWA schools. Such formative assessments were observed in about half of the classes in UNRWA schools in Gaza.

UNRWA Schools Successfully Create a Community and Culture of Learning

UNRWA's positive learning outcomes seem to be supported by a close interaction between school and community actors, as revealed in the qualitative data for this study. UNRWA schools have become key entities that form part of a broader culture of learning for Palestine refugees. Education provides meaning and relevance for children and youth in contexts of adversity. This is grounded in close interactions among parents, family members, teachers, and principals. Such school–community structures seem to evolve organically and are supported by classroom practice, school management, and system priorities (through explicit policies, rules, institutions, and dedicated resources). The resilience lens used to analyze data from student interviews identified five mechanisms in UNRWA schools that promote learning in the face of difficult living situations.

Education Provides a Collective Meaning and Purpose for Palestine Refugees in the Face of Adversity

For the Palestine refugee community, with more than 60 years of experience facing various causes of adversity, parental and community participation in school seems to be collectively valued and expected. This collective participation in quality education appears to have evolved as a way to face the difficulties experienced as a community. Students referred time and again to the social, cultural, and economic importance of being well educated, as noted in the following indicative responses:

> What motivates me is that I have a goal in my life, which is to become a doctor and work here and serve my country, Gaza-Palestine. I want to become an important person in the society, and being a doctor means being an important person in our society.
>
> Male student, Gaza

> What drives me to learn is that I want to be an engineer or a doctor; and I don't want to be like my father, without a job or a certificate; and to improve the situation in my home, and increase my country's level.
>
> Male student, Jordan

> School is a place where we come to learn in order to achieve our goals in life, especially since we are under occupation. I tell all occupied countries that knowledge is the only way to face occupation.
>
> Female student, West Bank

UNRWA Staff Understand and Are Able to Model a Positive Identity and Well-Being for Their Students in the Midst of Challenge

The sense of community appears to be strengthened by the fact that UNRWA teachers originate from the same at-risk population, are part of the same communities as students, and have themselves been through the UNRWA system. In sharing these difficult living situations, teachers are accessible role models for their students, providing them with motivation, a sense of responsibility, and kindness and support in times of need. Students recognize and value their teachers' understanding and assistance in times of need. Teachers, therefore, provide real-life examples to demonstrate that education can contribute to a person's identity and well-being in times of adversity. As one girl in Jordan explains:

> For me, when I see my teachers, I wish to be one of them. … I wish to be one of the teachers. When I look at a teacher, I ask: What made her reach this level? I'm sure she studied, and it was hard. Our computer teacher … always encourages us; she gives us advice on how to study, and when I follow it, I achieve what I want. … I want to say that when I look at my teacher, I wish to become like her.

The School System Supports Students' Competence in the Midst of Adversity through Academic Guidance and Socioemotional Support

Effective teaching strategies require socioemotional support and a caring and supportive environment in which to learn. This dual integrated focus on academic and affective guidance provides students with a sense of control and competence through education, which they see as relevant to their contexts. A nondualistic approach to education that integrates knowledge and values also appears to reflect the longer-term guiding principles espoused by UNRWA (a vision of empowerment and human development). This was aptly expressed by a female student in Jordan:

> Teaching is an essential thing. I have been at this school since first grade now. Teaching is really important and so is meeting other classmates and making friends. When it comes to the headmistress, she cares about discipline, psychological support, and students being responsible. When it comes to teachers, they always support us psychologically, teach us how to study, help us with our homework, help our mothers, set plans for exams, and prepare our lessons. In general, they guide us in many useful ways so we can study well.
>
> Female student, Jordan

Learning Is Supported by Many Actors Including Teachers, Students, Peers, and Family Members

Because UNRWA serves a refugee community, relations between school staff and families extend beyond the boundaries of the school campus. Students report multiple sources of support in their learning through these relationships, especially from family members and peers. This echoes much of what is well known about healthy child development (figure ES.7). Such community participation in the UNRWA system implies a wider organic process—beyond traditional top-down structures and models for school management.

UNRWA's Close Partnership with the Refugee Community Creates Shared Accountability for Learning Outcomes

Within the explicit references made by students on the varied roles school and community actors played to ensure a quality learning experience, they also

Figure ES.7   Students Benefit from a Wide Range of Support That Helps Them Learn despite the Adversity (Noting the Number of Times a Topic Was Mentioned in Student Interviews)

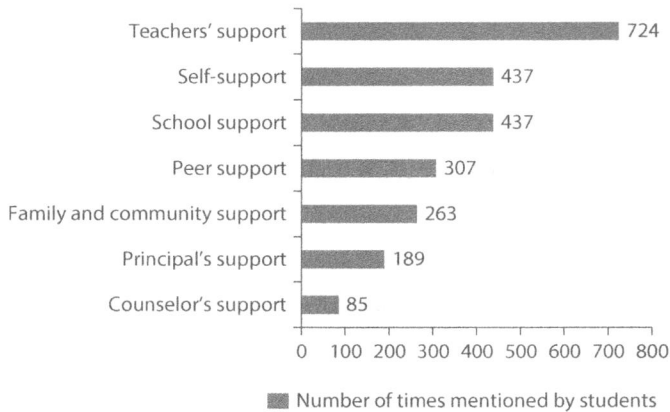

Source: World Bank interviews with students 2011.

pointed to a sense of mutual accountability across the classroom, school, household, community, and even society. In this way, UNRWA exemplifies a shared and reciprocal accountability for education by monitoring and supporting each other's actions:

> *Interviewer:* Do you have any thoughts, notes, or recommendations that will help you reach the highest levels of education, regardless of the difficulties that you talked about?

> *Student:* Provide a safe environment for the whole society—family, teachers, classmates, and neighbors. Simplify the lessons by explaining them in detail, and through hard work, I will learn and reach the highest levels of education.

UNRWA's performance in an adverse context (occupation, armed conflict, restricted movement, and protracted displacement) presents important lessons for other school systems. Specifically, the effective classroom practices of teachers, strong school leadership, sound assessment system, and shared accountability for learning are strong features. Equally important is recognizing the risks and vulnerabilities that students face and fostering relevant interactions across school and community actors to support learning and protection of students in such challenging contexts.

The five main lessons stemming from the study include the following:

1. Adequate teacher preparation appears to be a differentiating factor, but more can be done to expand on pedagogical innovations in the classroom.
2. Public schools in Jordan and the West Bank and Gaza can learn from the UNRWA system of assessment and accountability, as well as its teacher preparation and mentoring.

3. The fluctuating performance of UNRWA schools (as seen in the TIMSS 2011 results) is affected by rapidly changing contexts of adversity and continues to be of concern. Although UNRWA is successful in many ways and appears to provide relevant classroom- and system-level support, more is needed to strengthen this process to manage (downward) performance fluctuations over time. This also points to the fact that addressing the external sources of adversity is paramount.

4. Other countries can build on the UNRWA model to create a community and culture of learning that recognizes the adversity of vulnerable groups and promotes collaboration among the school, the teacher, the parent, and the community, all focusing on student achievement and well-being.

5. The UNRWA example highlights the need to understand education resilience as a process phenomenon which may be gauged and subsequently promoted by a set of assets and opportunities across a school–family–community partnerships. Resilience theory offers a better understanding of how education systems can achieve this for a given at-risk population, while concentrating efforts to end any structural causes of adversity.

As noted, this study highlights the existing value added for learning in UNRWA. Of course, there are other areas that can and should be improved. However, the assets identified in this study are a strong foundation for any future reforms. Especially for the UNRWA fields with the highest levels of adversity, such as the West Bank and Gaza, the factors identified seem to contribute to the resilient functioning of schools.

Note

1. Please see the appendix for detailed methodology.

Learning in the Face of Adversity • http://dx.doi.org/10.1596/978-1-4648-0706-0

Abbreviations

ICT	Information and Communications Technology
IEA	International Association for the Evaluation of Educational Achievement
ISCED	International Standard Classification of Education
NAfKE	National Assessment for Knowledge Economy Skills
NCHRD	National Centre for Human Resources Development
OECD	Organisation for Economic Co-operation and Development
PISA	Programme for International Student Assessment
PSM	Propensity Score Matching
SABER	Systems Approach for Better Education Results
TIMSS	Trends in International Mathematics and Science Study
UN	United Nations
UNESCO	United Nations Educational, Scientific, and Cultural Organization
UNGA	United Nations General Assembly
UNRWA	United Nations Relief and Works Agency

CHAPTER 1

The UNRWA Effect

Introduction

The United Nations Relief and Works Agency (UNRWA) is a regional United Nations (UN) agency with a quasi-state function to provide basic education, health, relief, shelter, microfinance, and community support to about 4.7 million registered Palestine refugees in the West Bank and Gaza, Jordan, Lebanon, and the Syrian Arab Republic.

In the aftermath of the 1948 Arab-Israeli war, which forcibly displaced more than 700,000 Palestinians, the United Nations General Assembly (UNGA) sought to mitigate the humanitarian impact of the crisis and work toward a long-term political solution. UNRWA, established as part of this response, began operations in 1950.

The agency was envisaged as a temporary "stopgap" measure to cater to refugee needs until a political solution could be reached (see box 1.1 for a definition of the UNRWA refugees). It was also established as one component of a wider special regime for assistance, protection, and reparations for the

---

Box 1.1 Who Are the UNRWA Palestine Refugees?

A refugee status for UNRWA responds to a very specific definition. In 1952, UNRWA defined its beneficiaries as "any person whose normal place of residence was Palestine during the period from June 1, 1946 to May 15, 1948 and who lost both home and livelihood as a result of the 1948 conflict." UNRWA registered refugees are officially known as "Palestine refugees." This definition excludes those who fled, were not deemed to be in need, or fled to areas outside of UNRWA's five areas of operations. Nor are refugee women able to retain or pass on their status to their children if they marry a nonrefugee. Only refugees in 1948 are officially covered by the agency, despite successive waves of displacement since then. Descendants of male UNRWA refugees do, however, inherit UNRWA's administrative title.

Source: Bocco 2010.

---

refugees as defined under UNGA Res. 194 (III). Its specific task was to implement "public works" programs aimed at the economic integration of refugees. But it began operations by taking over the ongoing emergency relief activities for the refugees, and 60 years later, it remains the only UN agency dedicated to meeting the needs of a specific population of refugees in a given region. Over the years, adaptations of UNRWA's services have been made possible by its flexible mandate, which facilitates rather than restricts the agency in its activities.

UNRWA's education program shares and in many ways defines this history because it was quickly established as a priority for UNRWA, and it remains the most significant program. It was also set up through a partnership with the United Nations Educational, Scientific, and Cultural Organization (UNESCO) that continues to this day, with UNESCO providing technical support through the funding of several key staff posts. The education program is managed by the Administration and Governance Unit at UNRWA headquarters.

Implementation is decentralized and based on project or program cycle management. Planning occurs in a fairly short time frame, and the various components are strategically linked to each other through a common and harmonized framework of results. The current strategy for service delivery (for 2011–15) is set out in UNRWA's Medium-Term Strategy, the "blueprint for programmes and field operations." The strategy provides the objectives, priorities, reforms, and new approaches for a six-year period, broken down into three biennia. These are in turn operationalized through Field Implementation Plans and Headquarter Implementation Plans. Across all of the strategy documents, the baselines, targets, and goals are expressed in terms of human development. Reflecting UNRWA's temporary status, it is funded through voluntary contributions of any amount from member states, which account for 95 percent of UNRWA's income.

A Brief Introduction to UNRWA: Evidence from Test Scores

The United Nations Relief and Works Agency (UNRWA) schools' results in international tests present something of an education system paradox that merits further study. Specifically, an econometric analysis of available achievement data concurs that UNRWA students have a competitive advantage over students in public schools. Observed characteristics related to schools, teachers, and students using an estimated education production function explain some of the differences in learning outcomes. Differences nevertheless persist even after matching. Finally, regression decomposition supports the conclusion that while contextual factors explain part of the variation in scores, a significant part remains unexplained and more "latent" factors need to be uncovered to support our understanding. Photo 1.1 shows students learning in a classroom in Palestine.

Photo 1.1 Students learning in a classroom in Palestine. © UNRWA Photo Gallery. Used with permission; further permission required for reuse.

UNRWA Schools Continually and Consistently Outperform Public Schools by a Margin Equivalent to More than One Additional Year of Learning

Econometric analysis shows a significant difference in test scores between UNRWA schools and public schools in Jordan and the West Bank and Gaza. Evidence for the analysis comes from several years[1] of Trends in International Mathematics and Science Study (TIMSS), Programme for International Student Assessment (PISA), and national assessment results. In all cases, UNRWA schools in Jordan and the West Bank and Gaza outperformed public schools. Notably, on the 2007 TIMSS assessment, UNRWA students in Jordan scored 494 and 541 points in math and science, respectively, compared with 427 and 482 points by public school students, more than two-thirds of a standard deviation higher and representing a significant difference in education outcomes. Also in 2007, UNRWA students in Jordan achieved close to the international mean in math and above the international mean in science. In the West Bank and Gaza, UNRWA students scored 381 and 414 points in math and science, respectively, compared with 367 and 404 by public school students and showed more significant differences in Gaza. Given UNRWA's status as an education system run for refugees, many of whom live in socioeconomic difficulty and contexts of ongoing violence and conflict, this merits further exploration and understanding. Specifically, the assessment data were analyzed with modeling techniques to identify factors that contribute to the difference in performance between the two school systems, as well as to measure the levels of explained and unexplained variation between them.

Learning in the Face of Adversity • http://dx.doi.org/10.1596/978-1-4648-0706-0

Box 1.2   Data Modeling Method Used in the Study

Mathematics and science scores are modeled against school type and characteristics, as shown here:

$$Y_{2007} = \beta_0 + \beta_1 \text{Type} + \beta_2 \text{School} + \beta_3 \text{Teaching} + \beta_4 \text{Student} + \beta_5 \text{Interaction} + \varepsilon$$

where Y_{2007} represents individual student test scores in TIMSS 2007, β_0 is the constant, β_1 is the coefficient for attending UNRWA schools, β_2 represents the coefficient for school characteristics, β_3 represents the coefficient for teacher characteristics, β_4 is the coefficient for student characteristics such as mother's education or socioeconomic characteristics, β_5 is used to assess how the school type is interacting with the different factors to affect scores, and ε is an error term.

Regression analysis was used to first test the degree to which school factors, teaching characteristics, and family factors explain the differences observed in the student achievement of UNRWA and public schools. Iterative regression steps were then used to demonstrate the association between school type and performance. After each iteration, controlling for school location and socioeconomic characteristics, the change in the magnitude and significance of the coefficient for school type was assessed (box 1.2).

It is important to keep in mind the UNRWA student selection criteria, because UNRWA students have to possess a refugee identification card to enroll. Students in possession of a refugee identification document cannot be refused enrollment in UNRWA schools, although they also have the option to enroll in public schools in Jordan and the West Bank and Gaza. However, Jordanians and nonrefugee Palestinians whose families are not registered as having been displaced in 1948 cannot enroll in UNRWA schools except in special circumstances (occasionally made if there are no public schools available in the area for nonrefugees). Thus, there is no "selection" into UNRWA schools.

Beyond this criterion, the 2007 results showed no major differences in background characteristics between UNRWA and public school students. This is corroborated by similarities in the wealth index[2] based on overall family possessions and the level of education of students' mothers. Overall, in the West Bank and Gaza, UNRWA students are slightly poorer, but their mothers are slightly more educated than their peers in public school (table 1.1).

At Baseline (without Controls) UNRWA Schools Increase Student Performance

In terms of the curriculum, UNRWA students consistently outperform their peers in math and science at public schools in Jordan and in the West Bank and Gaza (figure 1.1). These results are based on comparative evidence

Table 1.1 Student Background Characteristics, Based on TIMSS 2007 Data

Comparisons	Jordan		West Bank and Gaza	
	Public	UNRWA	Public	UNRWA
Age (years)	13.39	13.40	14.01	14.05
Female (%)	50	51	49	53
Mother's education (%)				
Primary/no school	19	17	25	12[a]
Lower secondary	14	11	19	19
Upper secondary	35	35	34	42[a]
Vocational	18	24[a]	9	12
Tertiary	14	14	13	15
Wealth index	−0.22	−0.26	3	−0.07[a]

Source: TIMSS study 2007.
a. Indicates statistical difference, $P < 0.05$. UNRWA United Nations Relief and Works Agency.

Figure 1.1 Comparison of TIMSS Scores over Time

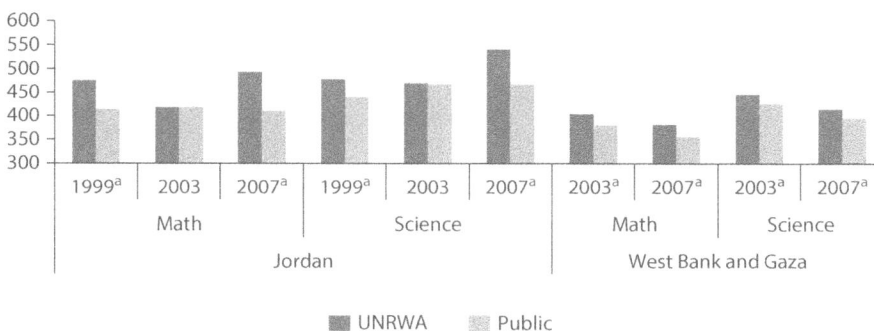

Sources: TIMSS studies 1999, 2003, and 2007.
Note: a. Statistically significant. UNRWA United Nations Relief and Works Agency.

from TIMSS, which helps demonstrate the extent to which eighth grade students have mastered curriculum content in mathematics and science that is common across participating countries. Only in 2003, in Jordan, was the difference between UNRWA and public schools not statistically significant.[3]

In terms of skills and competencies, UNRWA students consistently outperformed their peers in public schools in Jordan based on PISA (figure 1.2). PISA assesses whether 15-year-old students in participating countries can apply their knowledge and competencies in reading, mathematics, and science to real-world situations. The West Bank and Gaza do not participate in PISA.

Figure 1.2   Comparison of PISA Scores between Public and UNRWA Schools for Jordan

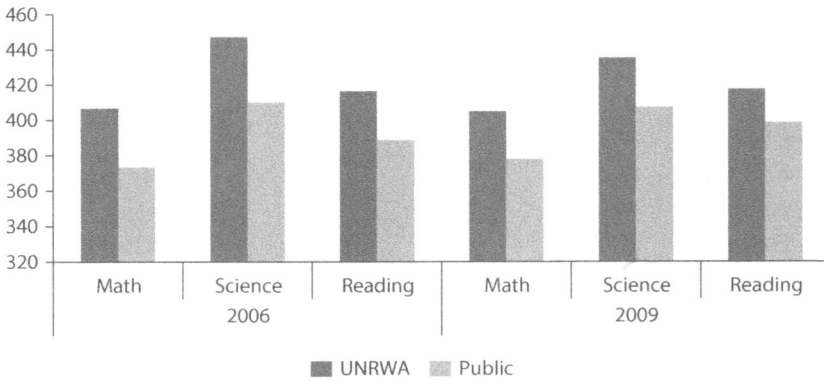

Sources: PISA 2006 and 2009 data.
Note: UNRWA United Nations Relief and Works Agency.

Figure 1.3   UNRWA Advantage: Magnitude of the Difference in Mean Scores Relative to Public in NAfKE (Jordan)

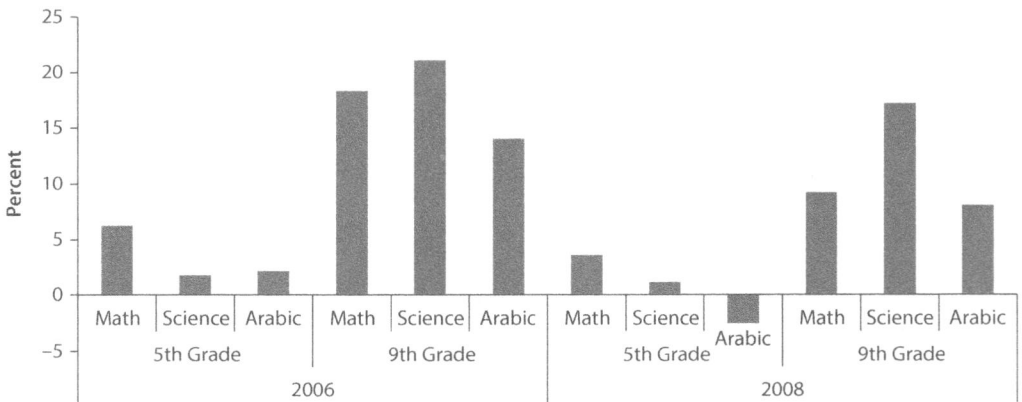

Sources: National Assessment for Knowledge Economy (NafKE) and National Centre for Human Resources Development, Jordan, 2008.

Finally, in terms of knowledge economy abilities, UNRWA students demonstrate their advantage in terms of a Jordanian national assessment instrument to test students' abilities in skills required for a knowledge economy (known as the National Assessment for Knowledge Economy Skills [NAfKE]).[4] NAfKE assesses student skill domains related to communication and problem solving. The results of NAfKE's 2006 and 2008 implementation for students in grades 5 and 9 (UNRWA does not have grade 11) were considered, and scoring relates to the percentage of test items answered correctly. Findings were similar to those of TIMSS and PISA; however, with the exception of math 2006 scores, the major differences occurred at higher grade levels. Students in UNRWA schools significantly outperformed their peers in public schools especially at grade 9 (end of cycle for UNRWA) in all content domains: Arabic, math, and science. On average, UNRWA students had scores one-fifth of a standard deviation higher than the scores of their peers in public schools. This suggests that students graduating from the UNRWA system have higher work-related skills than students graduating from public schools. Figure 1.3 shows the differences in test scores between the two systems in the two years of NAfKE implementation. Similar results are present in the national assessment in the West Bank and Gaza.

Performance of UNRWA Students Is Higher than Their Peers despite Two Important Characteristics

According to PISA 2009, globally 60 percent of within-country variance in reading performance is explained by the economic, social, and cultural status of the student. Contrary to international evidence, the difference in achievement between UNRWA and public schools goes far beyond this. Although the general perception is that refugees have relatively less well-off socioeconomic backgrounds than nonrefugee peers, resulting in lower learning outcomes, the opposite is true in the West Bank and Gaza context. Notably, the school-type coefficient continues to be statistically significant, and UNRWA schools had a 40-point advantage after controlling for socioeconomic status of children. Similarly, the significant advantage continued after controlling for other characteristics, such as location and student gender (figure 1.4).

To what degree can this difference be explained once other school, teacher, and student characteristics are controlled for? Furthermore, how much of the difference in performance, to the advantage of UNRWA, is associated with UNRWA's teaching and learning environment, given that they teach the same curriculum? Possible reasons include that UNRWA schools tend to enrich the curriculum with programs and activities that are not implemented in public schools (as revealed by field visits to schools). Family commitment and participation in the learning process may be another reason (as suggested by mothers' education status).

Figure 1.4   Predicted Mean Score Difference between UNRWA Schools and Public Schools, Controlling for General School Characteristics

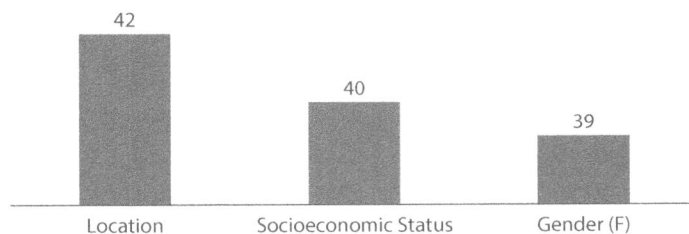

Source: TIMSS.

Do UNRWA Schools Increase Student Performance?

Although UNRWA schools use the same curriculum as public schools, differences are found in teachers' morale, training, support, and supervision. Using the teacher and the school questionnaires that accompany the TIMSS assessment, the differences between UNRWA and public schools in TIMSS 2007 were examined.[5] To ensure systematic variable selection, school visits and focus groups were conducted to then build a hypothesis for testing.

No significant differences are found between UNRWA and public school teachers' completed degrees. But on average UNRWA teachers report higher job satisfaction (75 percent compared to 51 percent) than their counterparts in public schools, and slightly more educators have a teaching certificate (81 percent compared to 76 percent).

Another important area of difference was the instructional time devoted to math and science at school. UNRWA students on average have slightly more hours per week of instructional time studying math and science. They dedicate more time to solving problems and are assigned more homework than their peers in public schools. Also, all UNRWA schools acknowledged that they offer enrichment or remedial classes. This is not the case for public school students. More significant differences were found in terms of school principals' perceptions related to parental support for education. UNRWA students have higher levels of parental support for student achievement and higher levels of parental involvement in school activities (table 1.2).

Various contextual factors that influence student learning were also tested to see if they explain some of the difference in scores between UNRWA and public schools. These factors include school, teacher, pedagogy, student, and home characteristics. In addition to location and general characteristics, overall school climate was considered (including the percentage of students who come from economically disadvantaged or affluent homes), whether or not the school offers enrichment and remedial courses in mathematics, and the frequency and severity of various problematic student behaviors occurring at the school. Teacher qualifications were also tested relative to their perceptions of job satisfaction, parental support and involvement, students' desire to do well in school, regard

Table 1.2 Comparison of Time Use and Level of Parental Support and Involvement

Comparison of time use and parental support	Public	UNRWA
Math time as percentage of total instruction time	13.5	15.0
Percentage of time spent in problem solving	31.8	37.0[a]
Math class hours per week	3.7	3.9
Frequency of math homework (weekly)	3.3	3.4
Parental support for student achievement (%)	0.13	0.51[a]
Parental involvement in school activities (%)	0.09	0.24[a]

Source: TIMSS Study 2007 data.
Note: a. Statistical significance. UNRWA = United Nations Relief and Works Agency.

for school property, how well prepared teachers feel to teach topics included in the TIMSS exam, and their expectations for student achievement. Pedagogical factors included percentage of time spent on problem solving, frequency with which the teachers ask students to do various content-related activities in mathematics and science, frequency and amount of homework, and frequency with which the teachers give tests or examinations.

As expected, these variables are positively correlated with learning outcomes. All correlations are statistically significant. (table 1.3 shows results based on separate regressions while controlling each for location, gender, and socioeconomic status.)

Finally, student factors included motivation in terms of their affinity for school, their perception of other students' motivation in school, of teachers' expectations for them, and of how much they like and feel competent in math and science, the importance and value they attribute to math and science, and the level of education they expect to complete. Student engagement and perceptions of feeling safe in terms of whether or not they were subject to problematic behaviors by other students were also included, along with the frequency with which they completed various learning activities and out-of-school activities (summarized by frequency with which a student participates in various nonacademic activities and homework outside of school).

Each of the contextual factors was divided into one of two subfactors: one that is changeable and could be adjusted by the education system for improvement and the other that is exogenous and beyond school influence. A stepwise regression method was implemented to monitor the changes in the magnitude and significance of school type (UNRWA or public) on performance. Tables 1.4 and 1.5

Table 1.3 Difference in Performance between High and Low Values in Characteristics Related to Teacher and School

Differences in performance	Coefficient[a]
Teacher has high expectations for students	29.9
Teacher has license or certificate	10.6
Participated in math training in the last two years	0.7
High job satisfaction	22.7
Math time as percentage of total instruction time	1.1
Percentage of time spent on problem solving	1.6
Math class hours per week	6.8
Frequency of math homework	10.6
High parental support for student achievement	50.0
High parental involvement in school activities	37.5
School offers enrichment classes	33.3
School offers remedial classes	19.0

Source: Regressions based on TIMSS 2007.
Note: a. All coefficients are statistically significant at $P < 0.05$.

Table 1.4 Results of the Regression Models (Jordan)

		Math						Science					
		Model						Model					
		0	1	2	3	4	5		0	1	2	3	4	5
	School type (UNRWA = 1, public = 0)	84.0ᵃ	77.0ᵃ	70.3ᵃ	63.2ᵃ	51.1ᵃ	48.6ᵃ	School type (UNRWA = 1, public = 0)	73.8ᵃ	68.0ᵃ	61.3ᵃ	55.4ᵃ	48.7ᵃ	43.2ᵃ
Student	Socioeconomic status		5.7	6.6	9.1ᵃ	7.3	6.4	SES		8.2ᵃ	7.9	10.8ᵃ	8.5	7.6
	Gender		18.2ᵃ	20.1ᵃ	23.4ᵃ	28.1ᵃ	26.5ᵃ	Gender		25.1ᵃ	26.6ᵃ	29.0ᵃ	31.3ᵃ	28.5ᵃ
	Motivated			5.8ᵃ				Motivated			8.2ᵃ			
	Proactive			4.9				Proactive			6.7ᵃ			
School	High percentage of students from economically disadvantaged homes				−3.9			High percentage of students from economically disadvantaged homes				−9.2ᵃ		
	School offers enrichment or remedial				6.7ᵃ			School offers enrichment or remedial				6.2		
	Severity of problematic student behaviors				−13.2ᵃ			Severity of problematic student behaviors				−16.3ᵃ		
Teacher	Qualification					2.5		Qualification					3.3	
	Confidence					5.8ᵃ		Confidence					6.1ᵃ	
	Job satisfaction					7.8ᵃ		Job Satisfaction					9.4ᵃ	
Pedagogy	Time as percentage of total instructional time						3.2	Time as percentage of total instructional time						2.6
	Problem solving						6.4ᵃ	Problem solving						5.2
	Assessment						7.8ᵃ	Assessment						7.2ᵃ
	Activities						4.4ᵃ	Activities						8.5ᵃ
	Homework						3.6	Homework						4.0
	R^2	0.10	0.13	0.16	0.19	0.28	0.34		0.11	0.14	0.19	0.22	0.29	0.37

Source: TIMSS 2007.
Note: Coefficients for student motivation, student proactive, school, teacher, and pedagogy are from the full model (model 5). UNRWA = United Nations Relief and Works Agency.
a. Statistical significance, $P < 0.05$.

Table 1.5 Results of Regression Models in the West Bank and Gaza

Math

		Model 1	Model 2	Model 3	Model 4	Model 5
UNRWA	School type (UNRWA = 1, public = 0)	35.1[a]	32.9[a]	30.3[a]	25.8[a]	23.4[a]
Student	SES	4.2	5.4	7.2	5.6	5.9
	Gender	20.6[a]	23.4[a]	24.6[a]	26.1[a]	25.4[a]
	Motivated		6.4[a]			
	Proactive		5.6			
School	Percentage of students from economically disadvantaged homes			−4.3		
	School offers enrichment or remedial			8.7[a]		
	Severity of problematic student behaviors			−15.1[a]		
Teacher	Qualification				3.6	
	Confidence				6.6[a]	
	Job satisfaction				8.6[a]	
Pedagogy	Time as percentage of total instructional time					1.2
	Problem solving					7.3[a]
	Assessment					6.1[a]
	Activities					4.1[a]
	Homework					2.5
	R^2	0.12	0.14	0.19	0.29	0.35

Science

		Model 1	Model 2	Model 3	Model 4	Model 5
UNRWA	School type (UNRWA = 1, public = 0)	40.2[a]	37.3[a]	35.8[a]	33.1[a]	28.6[a]
Student	SES	6.1	6.9[a]	5.8	4.7	7.2[a]
	Gender	28.5[a]	27.4[a]	26.0[a]	30.2	27.7
	Motivated		9.8[a]			
	Proactive		6.2[a]			
School	Percentage of students from economically disadvantaged homes			−7.5[a]		
	School offers enrichment or remedial			6.2		
	Severity of problematic student behaviors			−14.0[a]		
Teacher	Qualification				2.7	
	Confidence				5.7[a]	
	Job satisfaction				7.8[a]	
Pedagogy	Time as percentage of total instructional time					2.3
	Problem solving					4.3
	Assessment					5.0[a]
	Activities					6.6[a]
	Homework					4.7[a]
	R^2	0.15	0.17	0.23	0.36	0.41

Source: TIMSS 2007.

Note: Coefficients for student motivation, student proactive, school, teacher, and pedagogy are from the full model (model 5). UNRWA = United Nations Relief and Works Agency.

a. Statistical significance, $P < 0.05$.

show the different models for Jordan and the West Bank and Gaza, and the following represents the overall findings:

1. School type continued to be significant with additions of each of the contextual variables. Controlling for additional factors related to student, school, teacher, and pedagogy reduces the magnitude of the coefficient, but it continues to have a sizable and significant magnitude (between 23 and 42 points).
2. Student motivation and proactivity play a significant role in achievement.
3. Student behavior at school is crucial, and the increase in incidence of problematic misconduct has a major association with low performance at the school level.
4. Teacher qualification, in terms of the degree completed, did not demonstrate a significant association with student performance. However, their level of confidence to teach the subject was associated with an increase of about six points on the average student score.
5. Teacher job satisfaction played a significant role in explaining the differences in student achievement. A student taught by a teacher with high job satisfaction tended to achieve close to 10 points higher than a student taught by a teacher with low job satisfaction.
6. Although schools were not expected to have high variation in terms of instructional time, the difference in time allocated for math or science at the school did not indicate significance effects on achievement.
7. However, pedagogical activities, such as a focus on problem solving, testing, and practical activities in class showed a significant association with student achievement.

This Difference Is Confirmed under Additional Approaches

The propensity score matching (PSM) method was used to construct a matching group for every student attending UNRWA schools (possible observation under treatment). Then, performance on the different assessments was compared with the nontreatment group (for students attending public school). School and student characteristics were used to construct scores with which the matching is implemented.[6]

The positive effect of attending UNRWA schools decreases but remains statistically significant in Jordan, whereas in the West Bank and Gaza the positive effects are higher than the ones observed in a linear regression (table 1.6). It is important to note that the magnitude of the association is considerably high, especially in Jordan in 2007, when in math the estimate of the average treatment effect was 72 points and in science it was 65.

Similar results were seen for PISA in 2006; however, the difference disappeared in 2009 for math and reading (table 1.7).

Table 1.6 Comparison of Test Scores for TIMSS Controlling for Other Factors Using PSM

Country	Subject	Year	Without control		Controlling for other characteristics		Matching	
			Mean	P > |t|	Mean	P > |t|	Mean	P > |t|
Jordan	Math	1999	62.30	0.00	60.88	0.00	48.90	0.00
	Science	1999	37.72	0.00	35.18	0.00	31.23	0.00
	Math	2003	−0.25	0.98	−1.90	0.82	−5.62	0.63
	Science	2003	2.09	0.79	0.64	0.91	−0.12	0.83
	Math	2007	84.02	0.00	76.97	0.00	72.40	0.00
	Science	2007	73.76	0.00	68.04	0.00	64.65	0.00
West Bank and Gaza	Math	2003	24.02	0.00	20.73	0.00	12.79	0.00
	Science	2003	19.32	0.00	15.00	0.00	20.56	0.00
	Math	2007	25.21	0.00	17.50	0.04	20.63	0.01
	Science	2007	19.52	0.02	13.84	0.10	17.11	0.02

Source: TIMSS.

Table 1.7 Comparison of Test Scores for PISA Controlling for Other Factors and Using PSM (Jordan)

		Difference UNRWA—Public					
		Without control		Control		Matching	
Year	Subject	Mean	P > |t|	Mean	P > |t|	Mean	P > |t|
2006	Math	33.33	0.00	29.79	0.00	22.32	0.00
2006	Science	37.18	0.00	35.54	0.00	27.89	0.00
2006	Reading	27.75	0.00	24.37	0.01	15.20	0.02
2009	Math	27.05	0.07	23.09	0.07	17.09	0.26
2009	Science	27.93	0.06	26.46	0.03	26.93	0.09
2009	Reading	18.8	0.09	19.22	0.03	17.38	0.19

Sources: PISA 2006, 2009.

When using PSM for NAfKE, the difference remains significant in 2006, and in 2008 it is significant in science only for grade 9 (see table 1.8).

Thus, the results of the linear regression and the propensity scores matching analysis suggest that the difference in learning outcomes between UNRWA and public schools remain after controlling for other observed contextual factors. To estimate the magnitude of the explained variance associated with the observed characteristics relative to the unexplained difference between UNRWA

Table 1.8 Comparison of Test Scores for NAfKE Using PSM (Jordan)

			Difference UNRWA—Public					
			Without controls		Controls for family background		Matching	
Year	Subject	Grade	Mean	P > |t|	Mean	P > |t|	Mean	P > |t|
2006	Math	5	1.69	0.20	0.77	0.56	2.39	0.14
2006	Science	5	0.87	0.59	−1.89	0.29	−2.17	0.34
2006	Arabic	5	0.99	0.04	−5.38	0.01	−3.06	0.17
2006	Math	9	6.20	0.22	6.28	0.00	6.74	0.00
2006	Science	9	8.06	0.01	6.44	0.00	6.74	0.00
2006	Arabic	9	6.14	1.00	4.60	0.00	5.17	0.00
2008	Math	5	1.00	0.11	−0.58	0.62	−1.22	0.22
2008	Science	5	0.55	0.24	2.26	0.20	1.94	0.18
2008	Arabic	5	−1.22	0.03	0.23	0.91	1.08	0.72
2008	Math	9	3.43	0.77	3.79	0.00	1.74	0.26
2008	Science	9	7.36	0.43	7.62	0.00	5.3	0.00
2008	Arabic	9	4.2	0.00	3.29	0.03	1.9	0.17

Source: Calculations based on data from the National Centre for Human Resources Development Jordan 2009.

Box 1.3   The Model

The model specification used to estimate the production function for cognitive achievement is

$$T_{ij} = T(F_{ij}, S_{ij}) + \epsilon_{ij}$$

where T_{ij} is the observed test score (from the TIMSS math and science test) of student i in school j, F_{ij} is a vector of individual student characteristics, S_{ij} is a vector of school inputs, and ϵ_{ij} is an additive error, which includes omitted variables including those that relate to the history of past inputs, endowed mental capacity, and measurement error.

---

and public scores, the Oaxaca-Blinder decomposition method was utilized (see boxes 1.3 and 1.4).

At the End, Not All the Difference Is Explained

The observed test score differential can be decomposed as follows:

$$T_{UNRWA} - T_{PUBLIC} = (X_{UNRWA} - X_{PUBLIC}) \, \beta_{UNRWA} + X_{PUBLIC} \, (\beta_{UNRWA} - \beta_{PUBLIC})$$

where T is the standardized test score, X_i is a vector of student, and school-related characteristics for the i_{th} individual, β is a vector of coefficients, and *UNRWA* and *PUBLIC* subscripts are identifiers of the TIMSS test score in math

---

Box 1.4   Oaxaca-Blinder

This technique was originally used in labor economics to decompose earning gaps and to estimate the level of discrimination. It has been applied since to other social issues, including education. It is used in this study to assess how much of the achievement gap is due to differences in
characteristics (explained variation) and how much is due to the school and institutional characteristics that differentiates UNRWA from public schools (unexplained variation). This began with
a specification and estimation of the cognitive achievement production functions that relate
student achievement to individual and socioeconomic characteristics. The difference between
UNRWA and public schools is then decomposed into an explained component (to account for
student and family characteristics) and an unexplained component (that represents the school
and institutional variables), using the traditional Oaxaca-Blinder decomposition method.

Source: Blinder 1973; Oaxaca 1973.

Figure 1.5   Explained and Unexplained Portions of TIMSS Scores Based on Regression Decomposition

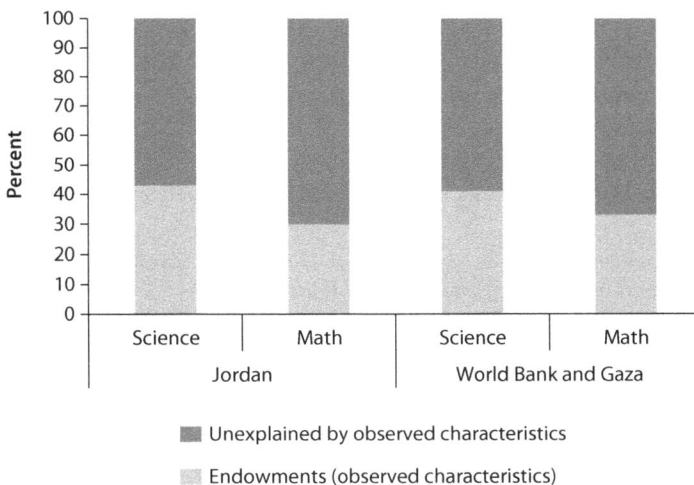

■ Unexplained by observed characteristics

▨ Endowments (observed characteristics)

Source: TIMSS Study 2007.

and science in 2007. The overall increase in test scores can, therefore, be decomposed into two components. One is the portion attributable to differences in
characteristics $X_{UNRWA} - X_{PUBLIC}$ or to the performance of the UNRWA group of
students X_{UNRWA}, and the other portion is attributable to differences in the
effects on performance $X_{UNRWA} - X_{PUBLIC}$ of public and UNRWA students
derived from the same characteristics. The second component is the unexplained
portion of the test score difference that may reflect certain unobserved family
characteristics that are correlated with achievement, possibly related to household wealth or perhaps due to school and institutional characteristics.

As shown in figure 1.5, the explained portion of the difference in test scores between UNRWA and public schools due to characteristics is between 30 and 40 percent. Hence, the majority of the difference is due to institutional characteristics and other factors. This leads us to believe that the largest part is most likely due to other institutional and individual factors beyond the observed inputs and socioeconomic characteristics of students.

To this end, further investigation of the overall system is needed. The next chapter identifies some of these factors that might shed light on the other piece of the explained variation in scores. An investigation of what happens in the classroom in the UNRWA schools relative to what occurs in the public schools is covered in chapter 3, and in chapter 4 those social and emotional supports (individual, community, and systematic) that support academic outcomes and the education resilience among refugee students are presented. Collectively, the findings present a more holistic view of UNRWA's learning model, which may explain some of the differences noted here.

Notes

1. 2011, 2007, and 2003 TIMSS for the West Bank and Gaza; Jordan also participated in 1999. Both Jordan and the West Bank and Gaza also implement national assessments. In addition, Jordan participated in PISA in 2006, 2009, and 2012.

2. For constructing the wealth index, we used the calculation methodology developed by Filmer and Pritchett (1998).

3. Focus group participants indicated that the drop in UNRWA's 2003 performance could be due to a management crisis that happened around the implementation of the field test.

4. NAfKE was developed in Jordan by the National Center for Human Resources Development in collaboration with the Ministry of Education.

5. We utilized 35 teacher questions and 22 school questions.

6. The scores are constructed by applying a standard probability logic model: $P_r\left(\frac{D_i}{X_i}\right) = \frac{e^{\lambda h(X_i)}}{1 + e^{\lambda h(X_i)}}$, where $h(X_i)$ is a function of covariates. The average treatment effect is then assessed, given the propensity score.

CHAPTER 2

Supporting Teachers and Managing Schools

The Systems Approach

The Systems Approach for Better Education Results (SABER) (box 2.1) and Stallings classroom observations method were used to compare public and United Nations Relief and Works Agency (UNRWA) systems in the policy areas of school autonomy and accountability, as well as teachers. Photo 2.1 shows a teacher and student in a classroom in Palestine.

UNRWA Teachers Are Better Supported

SABER-Teachers collected information on 10 core teacher policy areas by administering a set of questionnaires. The findings were then analyzed and education systems classified according to eight core teacher policy goals:

1. Setting clear expectations for teachers
2. Attracting the best into teaching
3. Preparing teachers with useful training and experience

Box 2.1 Systems Approach for Better Education Results (SABER)

SABER is a World Bank tool used to compare education policies and institutions. Data collected can help countries systematically strengthen their education systems, as it uses diagnostics to evaluate the quality of education policies against evidence-based global standards. Two SABER domains were used in this study to assess policies on teachers and school management and accountability and allowed for the classification of UNRWA and public education systems relative to their level of development around a set of policy goals.

Source: World Bank 2013c.

Photo 2.1 Teacher and student in a classroom in Palestine. © UNRWA. Used with permission; further permission required for reuse.

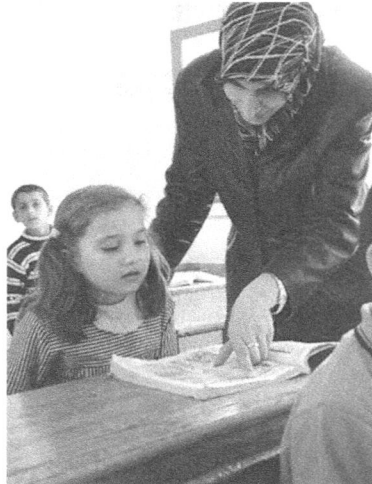

4. Matching teachers' skills with students' needs
5. Leading teachers with strong principals
6. Monitoring teaching and learning
7. Supporting teachers to improve instruction
8. Motivating teachers to perform.

Classifications were provided according to the metrics shown in Figure 2.1.

Figure 2.1 Metrics for Classifying Students

Latent	Emerging	Established	Advanced
●○○○	●●○○	●●●○	●●●●

The results show that overall, in terms of teacher policy and its implementation, the UNRWA system differentiated itself from the two public systems in four areas: (1) leading teachers with strong principals, (2) establishing strong and clear expectations for teachers, (3) monitoring teaching and learning, and (4) preparing teachers with useful training and experience.

UNRWA Is More Successful at Attracting and Recruiting High-Quality Teachers

While the public and UNRWA systems require the same level of education for recruited teachers, the UNRWA system differentiates itself in two areas, attracting the best into teaching and stringent requirements to become a teacher. UNRWA attracts the best high school graduates to enroll in the UNRWA

Table 2.1 Recruiting and Attracting High-Quality Teachers, UNRWA and Public Schools Comparison

Comparison of Successfully Recruiting and Attracting High-Quality Teachers	*Jordan Public*	*UNRWA*	*West Bank and Gaza Public*
Overall goal ratings	●●●○	●●●●	●●●○
Lever 1: Entry requirements set up to attract talented candidates?	Emerging	Advanced	Established
Lever 2: Teachers' pay appealing for talented candidates?	Established	Established	Established
Lever 3: Working conditions appealing for talented applicants?	Established	Advanced	Established
Lever 4: Attractive career opportunities?	Established	Established	Established

Source: World Bank 2012.
Note: UNRWA = United Nations Relief and Works Agency.

teacher colleges free of charge but with rigorous selection requirements. Attending the UNRWA teaching programs is very competitive as it targets high achievers on the high school national exam (*Tawjihi*). Also, before teachers are recruited at UNRWA schools they are interviewed and required to pass a written exam (see table 2.1).

There Are Clear Expectations about the Work Expected of UNRWA Teachers, Who Receive Guidance and Mentoring Services

UNRWA teachers are provided with explicit standards regarding what students must know and be able to do, and the tasks that teachers are expected to carry out are officially stipulated. Helpful guidance is given on the use of teachers' working time. Ninety percent of teachers' working time is dedicated to teaching whereas less than 60 percent of teachers' working time at public schools in Jordan is devoted to teaching. At the same time, at UNRWA schools teachers' official responsibilities include tasks related to instructional improvement with the help of a teacher mentor. The system also encourages teachers to support each other on school plans and design of curriculum material and to take part in the evaluation of activities (see table 2.2).

The focus on teachers also results in teachers who are more motivated to perform than their public school counterparts in Jordan and the West Bank and Gaza (see table 2.3).

The UNRWA system has a structured mechanism to hold teachers accountable. Teacher performance evaluations and professional development are requirements to remain in the field. Upon hiring, teachers are placed in a probation period during which mentoring and training is mandatory. After successful completion of the probation period, teachers are offered open-ended

Table 2.2 Teacher Expectations and Guidance, UNRWA and Public Schools Comparison

Comparisons	Jordan Public	UNRWA	West Bank and Gaza Public
Overall goal ratings	●●●○	●●●●	●●○○
Lever 1: Clear expectations for teachers?	Established	Advanced	Emerging
Lever 2: Useful guidance on the use of teachers' working time?	Established	Advanced	Emerging

Source: World Bank 2012.

Table 2.3 Teacher Motivation, Accountability, and Performance, UNRWA and Public Schools Comparison

Comparisons	Jordan Public	UNRWA	West Bank and Gaza Public
Overall goals	●●○○	●●●○	●○○○
Lever 1: Career opportunities linked to performance?	Emerging	Established	Latent
Lever 2: Mechanisms to hold teachers accountable?	Emerging	Established	Latent
Lever 3: Teacher compensation linked to performance?	Emerging	Established	Latent

Source: World Bank 2012.
Note: UNRWA = United Nations Relief and Works Agency.

appointments and are granted extra compensation based on performance. Teachers can also be dismissed for poor performance, absenteeism, or misconduct such as child abuse. In the UNRWA system, teachers' compensation is linked to performance through advancement and promotions from one level to another derived from an established ranking ladder. In the public system in Jordan, teacher classification exists (for example, beginner to master); however, promotion is based mainly on attending training programs and less on classroom performance and student learning as found in the UNRWA system.

UNRWA Has More Mandated Ongoing Professional Development and Orientation for Teachers

Although both public and UNRWA systems require at least ISCED5A[1] to become a primary school teacher, UNRWA also requires classroom experience. After recruitment, all new teachers must go through a mandatory intensive two-year structured training program that is focused on teaching and instructional practice (see table 2.4).

The SABER assessment also found that UNRWA teachers are better prepared in the area of improving their instructional practices. Of note, support for teachers is central in the supervision system established by UNRWA, especially

Table 2.4 Minimum Training Requirements for Teachers, UNRWA and Public Schools Comparison

Comparisons	Jordan Public	UNRWA	West Bank and Gaza Public
Overall goal ratings	●●●○	●●●●	●●●○
Lever 1: Minimum standards for preservice teaching education programs?	Advanced	Advanced	Established
Lever 2: Teacher entrants are required to be familiar with classroom practice?	Established	Advanced	Established

Source: World Bank 2012.
Note: UNRWA = United Nations Relief and Works Agency.

Table 2.5 Opportunities for Teacher Career Development, UNRWA and Public Schools Comparison

Comparisons	Jordan Public	UNRWA	West Bank and Gaza Public
Goal ratings	●●○○	●●●○	●●○○
Lever 1: Are there opportunities for professional development?	Emerging	Established	Emerging
Lever 2: Is teacher professional development collaborative and focused on instructional improvement?	Emerging	Established	Emerging
Lever 3: Is teacher professional development assigned based on perceived needs?	Emerging	Established	Emerging

Source: World Bank 2012.
Note: UNRWA = United Nations Relief and Works Agency.

during the beginning of their service. School principals are also mandated to ensure that teachers who need support are directed toward appropriate professional development programs or assigned mentors (see table 2.5).

With regard to matching teachers' skills with students' needs, no major differences were noted between the public systems in Jordan and the West Bank and Gaza and UNRWA. Each of the systems was found to be "established," offering similar incentives for teachers to work at hard-to-staff schools.

Teachers at UNRWA Schools Are Supported by Well-Qualified, Well-Prepared, and Experienced School Principals

The UNRWA system invests heavily in preparing and developing qualified school principals. Structured programs prepare and support school-based leadership

Table 2.6 Quality of School Principals, UNRWA and Public Schools Comparison

Comparison of Well-Qualified, Well-Prepared, and Experienced School Principals	Jordan Public	UNRWA	West Bank and Gaza Public
Overall goal ratings	●●○○	●●●○	●●○○
Lever 1: The education system invests in developing qualified school leaders?	Emerging	Established	Emerging
Lever 2: Principals are expected to support and improve instructional practice?	Emerging	Established	Emerging

Source: World Bank 2012.
Note: UNRWA = United Nations Relief and Works Agency.

through specific coursework activities and mentoring programs. UNRWA school principals tend also to have extensive experience before becoming school leaders, more so than in public schools. They are explicitly required to evaluate teacher performance and provide guidance for curriculum and teaching-related tasks (see table 2.6).

School Autonomy and Accountability Represent Areas for Improvement for Both

SABER-School Autonomy and Accountability was implemented to identify the depth and scope of programs and policies for school autonomy, learning assessment, and school accountability across UNRWA and the public system.

Overall, the SABER findings suggest little difference in terms of school autonomy and accountability between UNRWA schools and their public counterparts. Notably, with regard to financial autonomy,[2] both UNRWA and public systems have a centralized budget over which individual schools do not have much control (except for a small part of the operational budget). Nor were any major differences between the two systems noted in the area of school autonomy in personnel management. School principals do not have authority in hiring and firing decisions of teachers, as it is not managed by the school directors. Similarly, school councils (which may include the school principals) do not have legal authority to hire and fire teachers, nor to hire and fire a school director (box 2.2).

Finally, in terms of the participation of school councils in school finance matters, no major differences are found in relation to the role of school councils (where they exist) in budget planning and management, operational efficiency, and teacher incentives. This is because budgets are prepared at the central level outside of the influence of schools, and school councils do not extensively participate in assisting the school in the preparation of the school budget, nor do they have legal authority to approve budgets. At the same time, school councils

---

Box 2.2 What Matters in School Autonomy and Accountability?

The assessment of autonomy and accountability is based on the depth and scope of policies and programs linked to school-level control of financial and human resources, the depth and scope of parent and community participation in school management, and the depth and scope of school assessment and school accountability.

Emerging consensus on school performance indicates that school autonomy and accountability are key enabling factors for mobilizing individual incentives to teach and to learn (Barrera-Osorio, Fasih, and Patrinos 2009). By deepening school autonomy and accountability, schools can redefine their incentive structure to create better conditions for learning and teaching (Bruns, Filmer, and Patrinos 2011). Autonomy and accountability are also linked to assessment practices related to teachers and learning (Banerjee et al. 2010).

---

have no legal authority to supervise the implementation of the school budget, as it is the responsibility of central administration. In all areas, UNRWA and public schools were found to have a "latent" status.

The UNRWA System Has Fewer Management Layers and Is More Accountable for Student Outcomes

Despite the generally weak picture both systems present in terms of school accountability, some differences were noted in the UNRWA focus on the assessment of student learning, which was higher than that of the public system.

During their orientation, new UNRWA teachers are trained to assess student achievement, and overall assessment data are monitored by UNRWA "policy" makers. All major exams are prepared at the central level and are common across UNRWA schools in all fields of operation. Assessments are carried out in several ways including through standardized testing, inspections, and follow-up advice regarding identified issues at schools. Assessment findings are disseminated to teachers and used to identify schools and teachers who require additional support. The assessment data are also used to inform the development of teachers' lesson plans and support provided by the system in terms of instructional practices.

The UNRWA system also integrates a rigorous evaluation process as teachers are required to participate in internal and external monitoring and evaluation. Although both public and UNRWA evaluation systems include classroom observations and multicriteria reviews—covering knowledge of subject matter, teaching methods, student assessment methods, and student academic achievement—the evaluations are more rigorous and more frequent within the UNRWA system. In addition to their own assessment process, UNRWA schools also participate in national and international assessments, and the results of the school and student performance assessments are generally made available to parents.

Some of these differences also extend to the ways in which the UNRWA system assesses the mechanisms in place to render parents, local governments, and society accountable for education outcomes. UNRWA schools have manuals regulating the use of the results of the yearly assessments of school and student performance by school administrations or councils. Moreover, the assessment of school and student performance is part of a national and in some cases regional assessment system with results occasionally being used to compare school performance with schools in similar conditions (see table 2.7).

Conversely, in neither public nor UNRWA systems do school councils have the legal authority to hire external auditors to perform financial audits at the school. Given the important interconnections between different critical components of education systems in achieving quality learning outcomes, it will be important for UNRWA to build on these relative strengths.

Table 2.7 Management Layers and Accountability for Student Outcomes, UNRWA and Public Schools Comparison

Comparisons	Jordan Public	UNRWA	West Bank and Gaza Public
Overall goal ratings	●●○○	●●●○	●●○○
Lever 1: Are there systems in place to assess student learning to inform teaching and policy?	Emerging	Established	Emerging
Lever 2: Are there systems in place to monitor teacher performance?	Emerging	Established	Emerging
Lever 3: Are there multiple mechanisms to evaluate teacher performance?	Emerging	Established	Emerging

Source: World Bank 2011.
Note: UNRWA = United Nations Relief and Works Agency.

UNRWA Schools Promote High-Quality Teaching and Classroom Time

The Stallings Classroom Observation snapshot was used to study and compare instructional practices in UNRWA and public schools (box 2.3).

The data collected show that relative to advanced education systems (for example, those in Organisation for Economic Co-operation and Development [OECD] countries), the time spent on learning activities in both UNRWA and public systems in Jordan and the West Bank and Gaza is positively comparable. Significant class time (about 85 percent) is spent on learning activities. In the three regions, teachers in public schools spend similar amount of time on learning activities as in UNRWA schools (figure 2.2). Classroom instruction at UNRWA schools as well as at public schools includes a considerable amount of time on learning activities. Differences were noted, however, with regard to *how* this time is used.

Box 2.3 Stallings Classroom Observation

This data collection tool samples short time segments of classes in process. Known as the Classroom Snapshot ("snapshot" for short), it records every person in the classroom, what activities they are engaged in, and with whom they are engaged. Trained observers make a visual sweep of the classroom and view everybody and what they are doing and with whom they are doing it. The results are then recorded in a grid that includes all the possible adults (teacher, teacher aide, and visitor), all possible combinations of students (one, two, small groups, and large groups), and 15 categories of activities (including discussion, lecturing, assignments, social interaction, discipline, classroom management, and so on). The snapshot takes place 10 times during a class period.

Figure 2.2 International Comparisons in Teaching Time

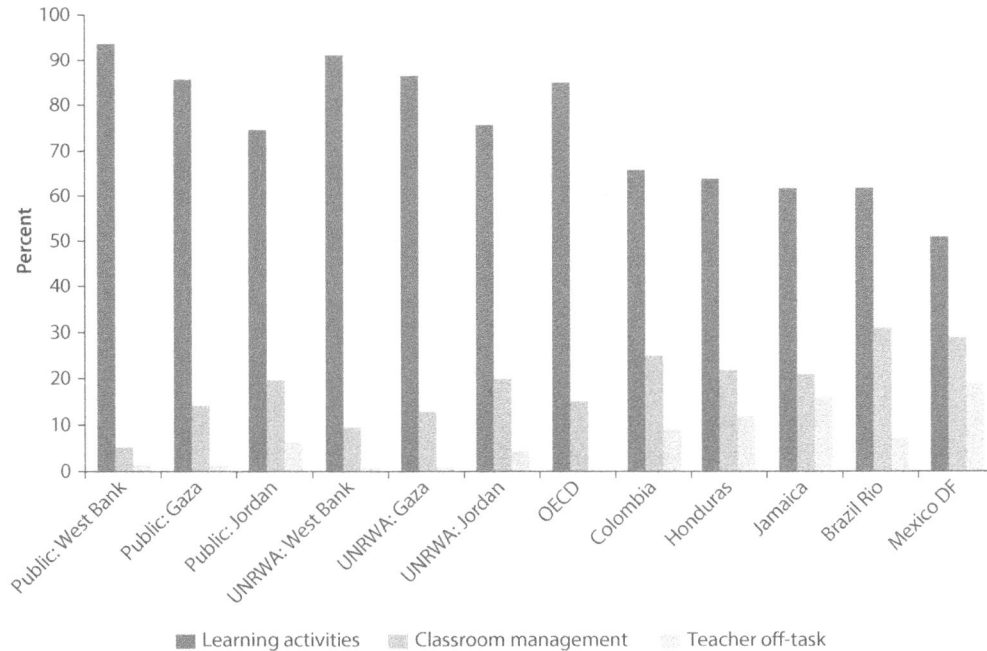

Learning activities   Classroom management   Teacher off-task

Sources: For public schools and UNRWA in the West Bank and Gaza, calculation based on classroom observations; for OECD and Latin America and the Caribbean, Bruns, Filmer, and Patrinos 2011; OECD data from Abadzi 2009.

There Is Less Waste of Teaching and Learning Time at UNRWA Schools

UNRWA classes dedicate more time for discussion and assignments than classes in public schools. Conversely, classes in public schools spent more time on lecturing and reading than in UNRWA schools. The UNRWA model includes more opportunities for students to engage with activities and writing. The trend at the public schools is more focused on the teacher and the textbook. Teachers in UNRWA schools are using teaching aids and information and communication technology (ICT) more than in public schools, and teachers utilize the displayed relevant material in the classroom (on the walls and tables). For example, all science classes in UNRWA schools are conducted in a science lab. Science is taught in regular classrooms in most public schools. Although less often in UNRWA schools, in both systems some students are off-task roughly a quarter to a third of class time.

Both the UNRWA and public systems include schools at different levels of instructional effectiveness. Signs of system effectiveness are highlighted by the higher percentage of competent teachers, as perceived by the observers, at the UNRWA schools. Additionally, snapshot observations reveal that UNRWA schools have less variation between schools and are more consistent in terms of instructional activities. This implies that pedagogical practices are more standardized in the UNRWA systems (likely through the preparation of teachers). This might also indicate effectiveness in teacher selection criteria (see figure 2.3).

Figure 2.3   Difference in Activities between Public and UNRWA Classrooms

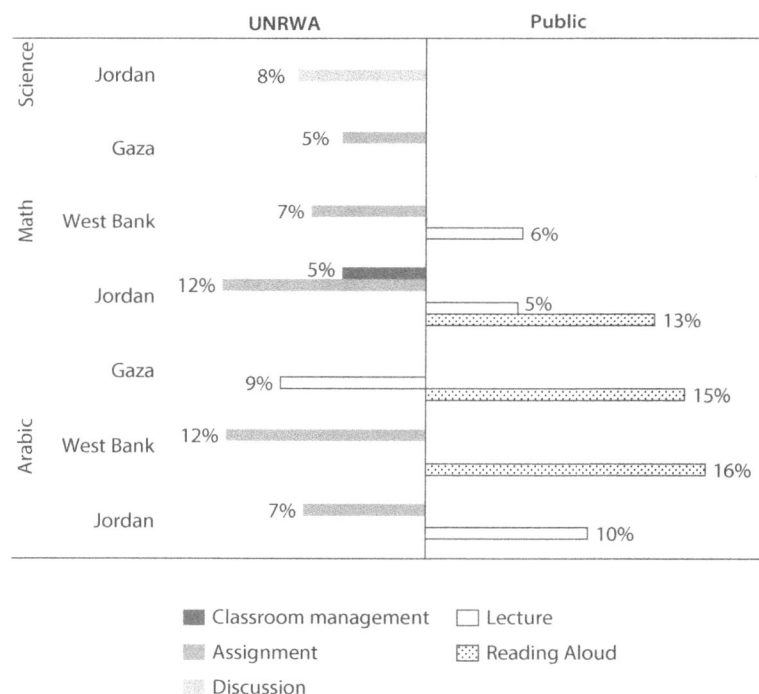

Although more could be done to improve the level of interactions in the classroom within UNRWA schools, observable indications suggest that the current pedagogical training and practices are something to build on in this respect.

Teacher Practices at UNRWA Schools Reflect a High Level of Confidence to Teach the Subject

Teachers and students in public schools read more from textbooks than in UNRWA schools. Students are writing and taking notes more in UNRWA schools than in public schools. Teachers in UNRWA schools use teaching aids and ICT more than in public schools whereas teachers in public schools spend more time writing on the blackboard. Figure 2.4 illustrates material use by region and school type.

Teachers in UNRWA Schools Implement More Activities, Discussions, and Assignments

Observable differences at the classroom level included higher levels of student engagement in UNRWA class activities (as a percentage of class time). This was

Figure 2.4   Important Difference Regarding the Use of Materials by School Type

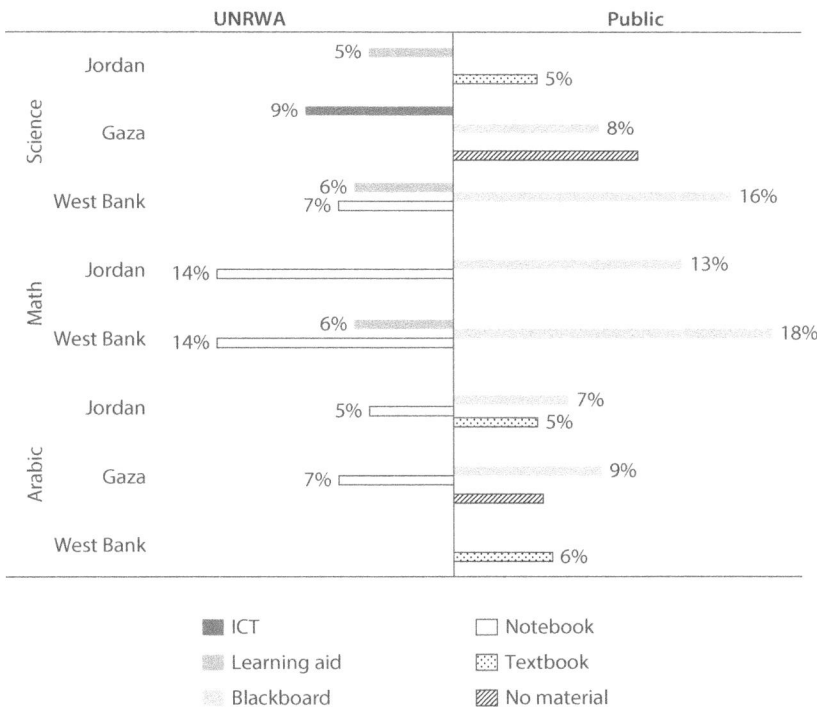

Source: Calculations based on classroom observations.
Note: ICT = information and communications technology; UNRWA = United Nations Relief and Works Agency.

most common in Jordan and Gaza across the three core subjects. However, there appears to be large variation within UNRWA schools, particularly West Bank versus Jordan and Gaza, which could be due to a variety of factors, including (1) UNRWA schools are more effective in some areas than others, or (2) public schools in the West Bank are becoming closer to UNRWA in these practices than in the other areas (see figure 2.5).

Figure 2.5 Percentage of Classes in Which Students Work on Measurable Activities

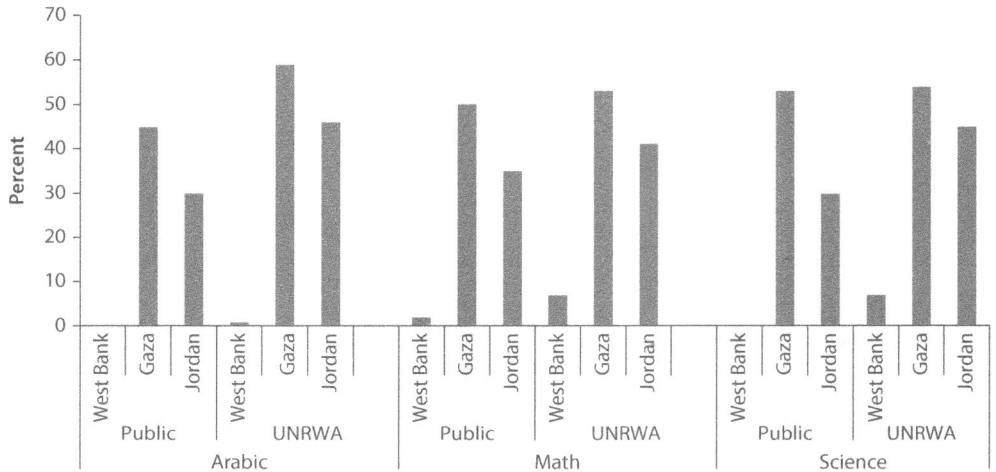

Source: Calculations based on classroom observations.
Note: UNRWA = United Nations Relief and Works Agency

Figure 2.6 Percentage of Classes with Quizzes or Test Preparation

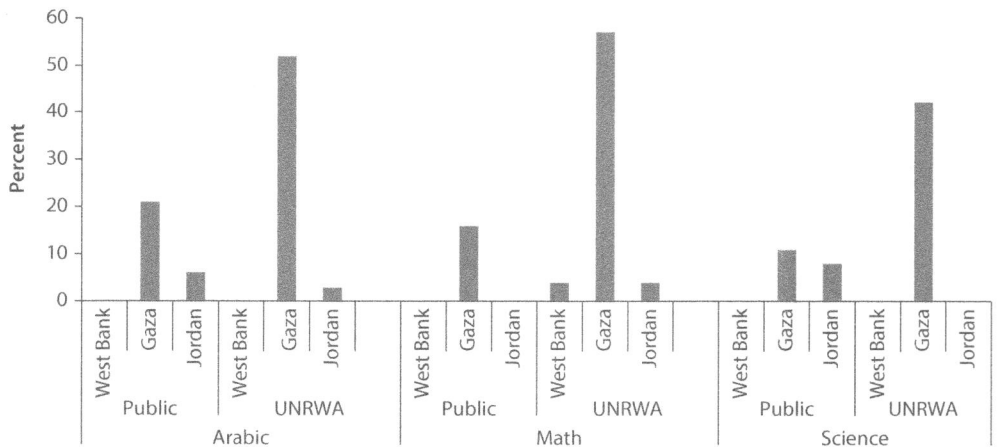

Source: Calculations based on classroom observations.
Note: UNRWA = United Nations Relief and Works Agency.

In some cases it was noted that UNRWA teachers provided students with practice tests or dedicated time to review and test preparation. This was most frequent in Gaza, where it was observed in about half the classes in UNRWA schools (figure 2.6).

This may help account for the lower incidence of students being off-task in UNRWA schools. The snapshots also measured the incidence of students who were not engaged in learning and were either socially interacting with other students or remained completely uninvolved in any classroom-based activity. Results show that overall the incidence of the latter two possibilities was 10 percent higher in public schools as compared to UNRWA schools. The difference between UNRWA and public schools was highest in Gaza and Jordan (figure 2.7).

Furthermore, at the end of each classroom observation, researchers were asked to provide an overall rating of the class and the teacher. The results presented in figure 2.8 show that in the areas of teacher competency and mastery of class content, UNRWA schools scored higher in comparison to public schools for all subjects observed.

Researchers also rated the overall lesson quality. This resulted in a lower rating for public schools, whereas the percentage of schools achieving a superior rating was higher in UNRWA schools (figure 2.9).

Figure 2.7   Incidence of Students Being Off-Task

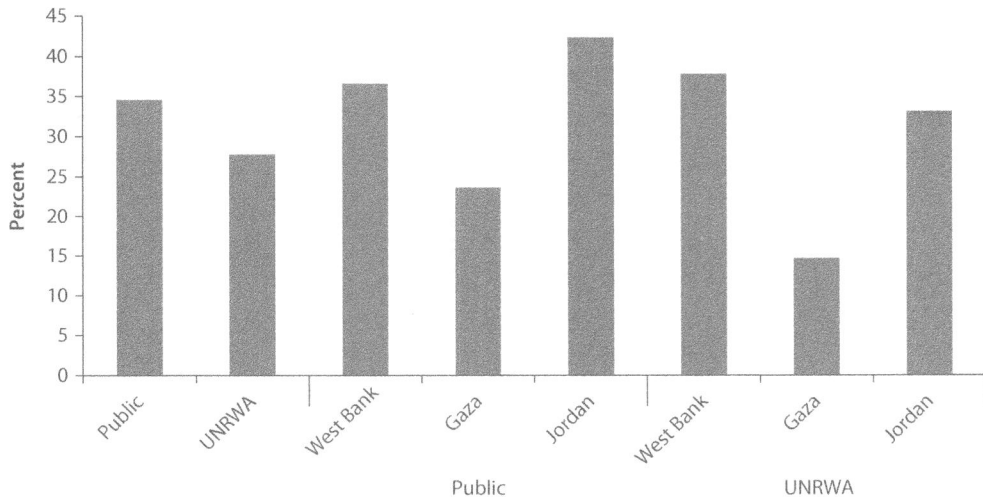

Source: Calculations based on classroom observations.
Note: UNRWA = United Nations Relief and Works Agency.

Figure 2.8   Rating of Teacher Competency by Region and Subject

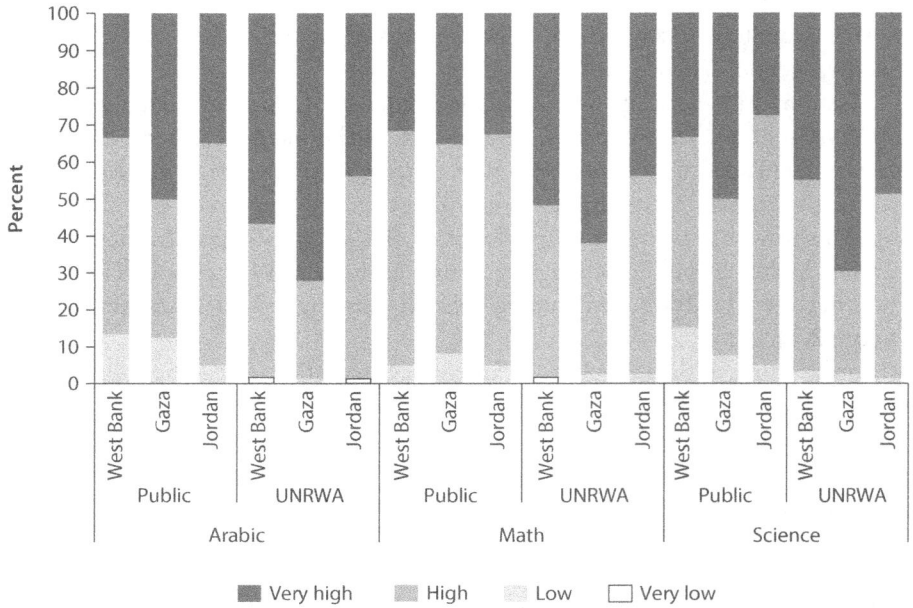

Source: Calculations.
Note: UNRWA = United Nations Relief and Works Agency.

Figure 2.9   Overall Lesson Quality by Region and Subject

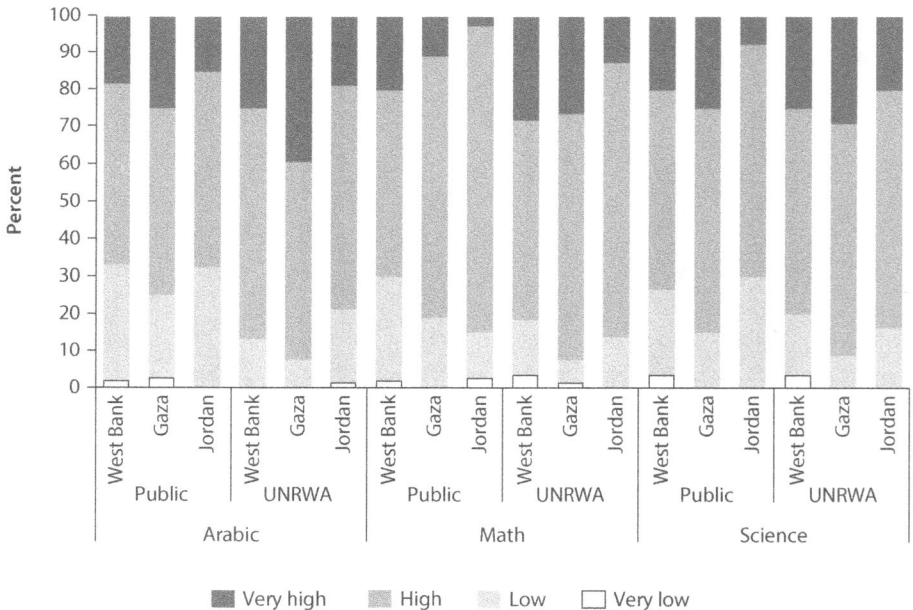

Source: Calculations.
Note: UNRWA = United Nations Relief and Works Agency.

Conclusion

Thus, based on our research we find that the UNRWA system is more successful at attracting and recruiting high-quality teachers; there are clear expectations about the work expected of UNRWA teachers, who receive guidance and mentoring activities. UNRWA also has more mandated ongoing professional development and orientation for teachers. These schools are well supported by well-qualified, well-prepared, and experienced school principals. The UNRWA system has fewer management layers and is more accountable for student outcomes. There is less waste of teaching and learning time, more interaction and student involvement in instruction, and teachers exhibit a high level of confidence in teaching their students. Overall, school autonomy and accountability represent areas for improvement across both UNRWA and public schools.

Notes

1. ISCED stands for International Standard Classification of Education; ISCED 5A means a Bachelor's degree.
2. School autonomy is defined as an increasing degree of local control of central fiscal transfers in terms of a school's having authority to manage its operational budget, set and manage staff and teacher salaries, or raise other funds in addition to the transfers received from national or subnational sources.

CHAPTER 3

Learning and Resilience

Introduction

The Palestine refugee youth interviewed for this study are aware of the adversities they face and expressed that education helps them maintain hope for the future (box 3.1). Finding a purpose to their learning is not only an individual choice but one promoted and supported by the wider community. Students, with the support of their teachers and their families, set feasible and pertinent personal and community-related goals for their education. School staff, family members, and peers provide academic and socioemotional support and are mutually accountable for results. Communities do not do this alone. The United Nations Relief and Works Agency (UNRWA) education system—imbued with the Palestinian refugee context—strives to offer relevant learning opportunities and equitable opportunities in pursuit of these goals. We call this multilayered process for achieving positive education outcomes in the midst of adversity "education resilience." Five education resilience supportive mechanisms were identified in UNRWA schools.

Box 3.1 Qualitative Data Approach

To understand the underlying mechanisms that UNRWA students considered important to learn in a context of adversity, the resilience evidence comes from a purposeful sample of 74 interviews. The students were selected for their good academic performance in spite of their relatively more difficult living situations in comparison to their peers.

The interviews provide important insights into *how* the students succeed and the individual-, community-, and system-level features that help them. The data are qualitative; the counts noted in some graphs are only contextual references to the number of times a topic was mentioned across interviews (it is not intended for statistical analysis).

Photo 3.1. Schoolgirls in Palestine. © UNRWA. Used with permission; further permission required for reuse.

Education Has a Collective Meaning and Purpose for Palestine Refugees in the Face of Adversity

Resilience starts from adversity. A wealth of data on the adversities faced by Palestine refugee students was collected through interviews. Students recognized the range of adversities they live under, which affected them in proximal ways when it came to learning. In other words, although the external context of armed conflict, violence, or being a refugee was well understood by the young people, its negative impact was felt in more tangible terms at home and in school. At home, students were affected by socioeconomic hardships—such as unemployed parents, incarcerated family members, and limited access to basic resources. At school, the external adverse context also impacted the day-to-day interactions they had with teachers and other students.

Paradoxically, adversity was also a motivating factor to do well in school. Indeed, when faced with particular episodes of adversity, many of the students noted how this merely provided an added impetus to succeed in their studies:

> Because my parents' divorce affected my learning, when I overcame this problem I decided that I wouldn't let any problem distract me from studying, and I made some rules to use if I encounter any problems so I won't let it affect my learning. I must solve these problems without allowing them to affect my education.
>
> Male student, West Bank

I can't describe the fear that we lived in … I was the only one at home who was studying for final exams. My father used to ask me when he saw me studying why I wasn't afraid. We all used to sit in the same room during the days of the war, and my father didn't go to work so we followed his lead, but studying for my exams was the most important thing for me to do especially during the days of the war.

Female student, Gaza

Education, in turn, played an important role in helping students to make sense of the adverse conditions within which they lived. They understood difficult life events as opportunities and education as protection. Education became the primary means through which they set tangible and realistic goals for themselves and in some cases in relation to the wider Palestine refugee community (figure 3.1). As one boy in Gaza noted:

My motivation is to get a good future, and to know my future lies and to put a goal in front of me. And I've put education as a goal in front of me and I have to do it, so I have to learn and to know all the subjects and to pay my attention to the teacher's explanation, and to have a better future.

Common goals were to become well-educated professionals such as doctors, engineers, and, significantly, teachers. These personal goals were often linked to a desire by students to be positive role models in their communities. This was neatly expressed by one female student in Gaza, who in recounting her experiences of the war noted:

I'm a good student although when I was at the fifth grade, the war began and my uncle died in that war; I felt that these days were like a test for us, the students, to work and study hard regardless the difficult days that we faced.

Figure 3.1 How Students Make Sense and Find Purpose through Education

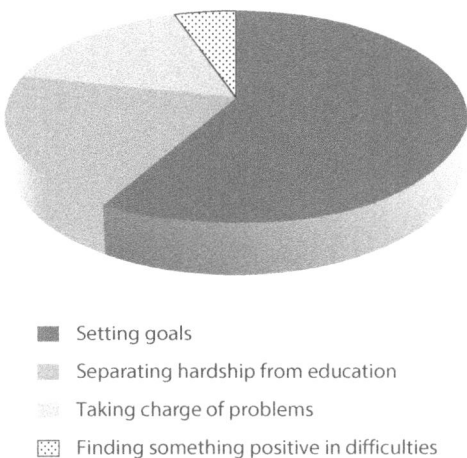

- Setting goals
- Separating hardship from education
- Taking charge of problems
- Finding something positive in difficulties

Learning in the Face of Adversity • http://dx.doi.org/10.1596/978-1-4648-0706-0

From the analysis of their narratives, a pattern emerged of students' awareness of the adversities associated with being Palestine refugees, but also of education helping them to maintain hope for the future. The UNRWA education system seems to offer learning opportunities that are meaningful to the lives of these students (relevant both to their situation as a marginalized refugee population and as individual students who have faced particular personal difficulties). Such positive values shape the identity of Palestine refugees and promote a sense of personal well-being and control, connection with others, and social accountability (figure 3.2). For example:

> I have one goal: to be a doctor or an engineer, so that we can show our enemy that even though we lived in difficulties, we became successful in our lives.
>
> Male student, Jordan

> *Interviewer:* Does being a Palestinian refugee have a positive or negative impact on you?
>
> *Student:* It urges me to study harder since we are refugees who had to leave their land and have to work hard to improve our status and prove our identity.
>
> Female student, West Bank

Figure 3.2   The Type of Goals High-Performing Students Relate with Doing Well in School (Disaggregated by Gender and Noting the Number of Times It Was Mentioned in Student Interviews)

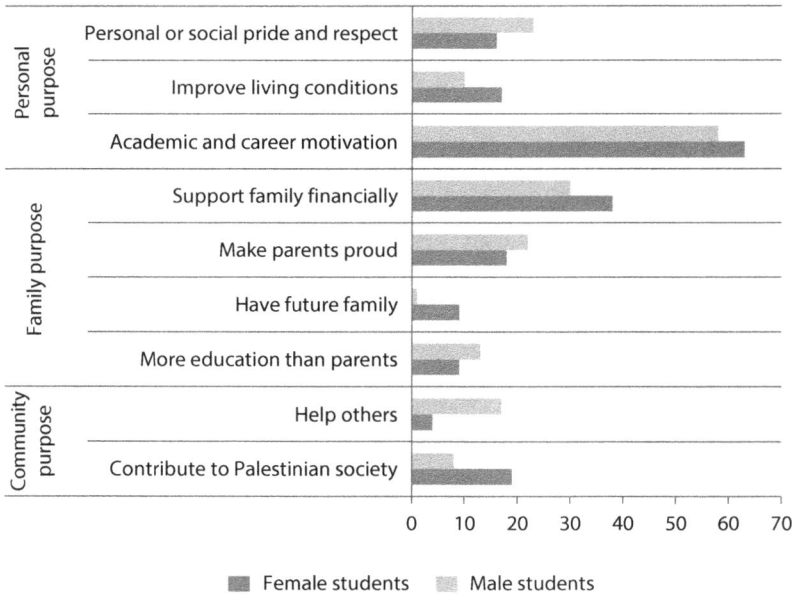

Source: Calculations based on student interviews 2012.

UNRWA Staff Understand and Are Able to Model a Positive Identity and Well-Being in the Midst of the Same Challenges Their Students Face

The high cultural premium for learning reflects a clear and unwavering prioritization of education, which is promoted at the school level by teaching staff. Teachers can provide effective support to students in adversity, especially when they understand the challenges faced. Many of the student narratives provided evidence of how teachers, head teachers, and counselors understood the challenges students confronted and were dedicated to addressing the potential negative impacts on learning. School staff were often noted to be very approachable and went above and beyond their professional duties to support students and ensure they were able to continue learning despite living and learning in a difficult context. This included a significant amount of out-of-class support as described by this female student in Gaza:

> We had a teacher in the sixth grade; she used to come to our home and teach me math every day. I was the smartest student in her class and always get the highest marks in math, and I'm still good at math thanks to her. Whenever I need help with any school subject even if it's not math, I go to her house.

Another boy in the West Bank spoke of how his English teacher was always on hand to help outside of class hours:

> He likes to joke with us during the class, but at the same time he's very good at teaching. He knows how to teach us and make us all understand, and if we have a difficulty with anything he would explain it to us during the class or after the class; we can go to him any time.

The motivation of UNRWA teachers and their ability to understand and connect with their students is not surprising. UNRWA teachers are themselves Palestine refugees and as such hail from the same at-risk population, are part of the same geographical communities as the youth, and have themselves been educated in the UNRWA system. They are committed to a community project of educating their youth and share and promote this goal in proximity with family members. For example, when asked about his parents checking on his school performance, one boy in the West Bank told us:

> Yes, my father always calls my teachers and the principal, and one of my teachers … knows my father and uncle very well, because he went to school with my father, so he always talks to my uncle about my performance at school, and my father sometimes calls him and visits him at school. That's how he checks on my performance at school.

A major benefit of school staff that share or have shared many of the same adversities as their students is that they have useful insights into their students' lives. Teachers can serve as role models of personal well-being and a positive identity. This was alluded to by one girl in Gaza, who told us:

> The best thing about my teachers is that they treat us like any normal student; they treat us like citizens who live in their own country; they always talk to us and tell us about our rights.

Students were acutely aware of the influence of teachers on their lives and told us that they often saw their teachers like a second family, while schools were also described in terms of being a second home. Students refer to this positive influence from their teachers as follows:

> For me, when I see my teachers, I wish to be one of them ... I wish to be one of the teachers. When I look at a teacher, I ask: What made her reach this level? I'm sure she studied and it was hard. Our computer teacher ... always encourages us, she gives us advice on how to study, and when I follow it, I achieve what I want. ... I want to say that when I look at my teacher, I wish I to become like her.
>
> Female student, Jordan

> *Interviewer:* What do you like in a teacher?
>
> *Student:* The way they educate the students and treat the student as his son or little brother.
>
> Male student, Gaza

As Bocco has stated relative to the UNRWA system, "the practice of teachers is embedded in their local experience: They themselves are refugees and share the same experiences of most pupils' parents" (Bocco 2010, 245). Yet, this connection between students and teachers is not necessarily unique to the UNRWA system. Rather UNRWA may be using this to its benefit as an agency that was specifically set up to manage the adversity experienced by the refugees. Its approach to education seems to recognize that context impacts the educational experiences of students, and vice versa.

The School System Supports Students' Competence in the Midst of Adversity through Academic Guidance and Socioemotional Support

Students reported that effective teaching in adversity comprised academic guidance and socioemotional support. As was noted in earlier chapters, academic guidance in UNRWA schools included effective teaching and learning practices (such as time on task and the use of supplementary materials and practical experiments), assessments (including practice exams), and accountability for results (which was achieved through high expectations for all students and recognition of their efforts). Interviewed students also noted the availability of equity-focused programs (which students referred to as remedial or catch up classes), and an orderly learning atmosphere (through discipline and a well-maintained learning environment).

For students, a good teacher, in terms of academic guidance, was one who provided multiple techniques to take students beyond a passive transfer of knowledge. A good teacher engaged students in critical and creative thinking and ensured that there was a sense of equality of opportunity among students. This was exemplified by the response of a male student in Gaza. When asked about what made a good teacher, he responded:

> That he can provide the information clearly and he doesn't differentiate between the students, and he should give us more than what is in the textbook to accommodate our ideas. He should give everything that is useful for the students, and help us with creativity and thinking, not only memorizing and following the textbooks word for word.

Other students stressed the importance of teachers being able to simplify or clarify topics for the class, ensuring that they did not depart from a lesson until everyone understood. For example, a male student in the West Bank explained why he liked learning English:

> It's an easy subject to learn; our teacher simplifies it for us and makes us like it. I like his teaching method; he explains the lesson and makes sure we all understand, and if there was anyone who didn't understand anything, he would explain everything to him.

Perhaps not surprisingly, students drew clear links between a teacher's ability and thus motivation to do well in a particular subject.

Figure 3.3 presents the varied forms of academic guidance that the students reported, including components that took place both within regular class time and outside of it (again speaking to the high levels of commitment and motivation of UNRWA teachers).

However, the above references to academic and cognitive skills were also complemented by the socioemotional support and important values students saw in a good teacher. Empathy, respect, and trust were common themes in the students' descriptions of effective teachers and head teachers. Students provided numerous examples of teachers providing them with personal guidance, acting as confidents, and helping them to address particularly difficult moments in their lives. Students respected this commitment, and it furthered their motivation to study hard and find purpose in education. For example, when speaking about the impact of conflict in Gaza, one girl explained:

> Teachers were with us all the time. They even visited us at home. That gave me a great motivation. It really feels good when you see that someone cares when you are in an ordeal.

Figure 3.3 Types of Academic Guidance Provided to Students (Noting the Number of Times a Topic Was Mentioned in Student Interviews)

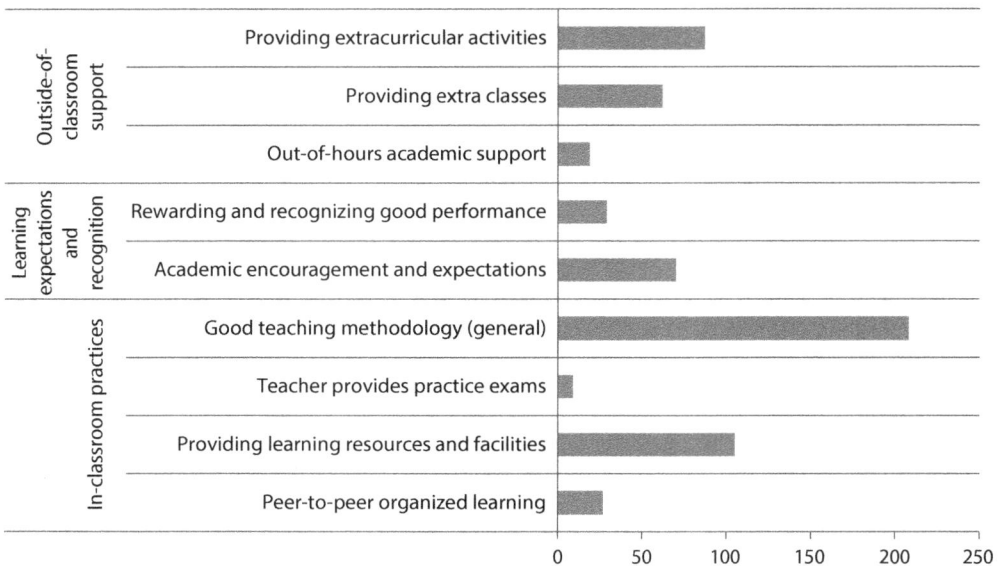

Source: Calculations based on student interviews 2012.

Reflective of this as well, a male student in the West Bank spoke of the dedication of his head teacher in supporting a fellow student whose father was in jail:

> One of my classmates' father was in prison for six years, and he was released nine months ago, and he didn't have a job but now he's working but he does not get paid enough. So the principal used to help him all the time, and sometimes when he [my classmate] had to visit his father at the prison, he would have to miss classes that day, so the students would go explain the lessons to him that he missed; they helped him with school and with his personal life.

Another illustration of social and emotional support comes from a female student in Jordan who, when asked about what teachers offered their students, responded:

> They give moral support. Concerning financial support, our religion teacher helps poor students; she raises money and gives it to the poor. Whatever donations come to school she would distribute them to the poor. Our English language teacher provides us with the necessary advice to become effective members in our country.

Yet, although it may be analytically possible to distinguish two types of support—academic guidance and socioemotional support—in practice they both formed an integrated approach to effective teaching and learning. For students this translated into a sense of protection, affable feelings toward their teachers, and sentiments of competence, motivation, and responsibility toward their studies. For example, a female student in Jordan remarked:

When I get a good mark like 30 out of 40, my teacher encourages me positively to get full marks for the next time and praises me before others. Thus, my participation becomes better. Moreover, whenever my answer is unique and not everyone is capable to answer the question, she rewards me with a simple gift, not necessarily an expensive one. Every teacher has her own style in motivating students and when a teacher is good with students, they love her in exchange and study well.

Students indeed noted that socioemotional interactions actually enhanced students' cognitive abilities to excel academically. This is captured in the following interview segments regarding how teachers help their students:

She is one of a kind. She says yes whatever you ask her for. She helps a lot whether you are sick or you have a problem at home. She also goes to give condolences along with teachers when a member of a student's family dies. That really affected students and encouraged the sense of belonging. They felt they have a value at their school and that makes them do better. There was a student who had lots of help from teachers and benefited a lot and did much better.

Female student in Gaza describing her school principal

There are many things that I like; you can see most of these things through the way they treat the students, through the ways they explain the lessons, through the way they run the class and manage it, and through the way they talk to students, get them to study, and get those students to come talk to them whenever they're facing problems.

Male student, Gaza, discussing what he likes about his teachers

Teaching is an essential thing. I have been at this school since first grade now. Teaching is so important as well as meeting other classmates and befriending them. Concerning the headmistress, she cares about discipline, psychological support, and students' honoring. Concerning teachers, they always support us psychologically, teach us how to study, do our homework, help our mothers, set plans to exams, and prepare our lessons. In general, they guide us to many useful ways concerning studying well.

Female student, Jordan

The integrated nature of academic guidance and socioemotional support points to the importance of not simply addressing these needs through parallel psychosocial programs but rather through incorporating noncognitive skills and values in the teaching and school management processes. Indeed, in the case of UNRWA, it appears that this integrated support is not simply born of individual initiative but is explicitly supported by the agency. This is, for example, reflected in the institutional prioritization of cross-cutting concerns such as gender, disability, youth, environment, and protection. Particularly germane to this study is UNRWA's focus on "protection" within its policies for "safeguarding and protecting the Rights of Palestine refugees" (UNRWA 2008). Within this approach, protection is conceived as an integral part of UNRWA's service delivery for which partnership with the community is an important element (UNRWA 2008). The emphasis on providing socioemotional support as a key component of quality education is also referenced in a recent education program communique entitled "education, learning together," in which UNRWA states:

> Providing a quality education for all young people will impart an understanding of their place in the world and convey a common set of key values such as dignity, tolerance, a sense of cultural identity, gender equality, human rights, and respect for the environment; while strengthening coping strategies, especially in a context where poverty pervades daily life (UNRWA n.d., 4).[1]

Learning Is Supported by Many Actors Including Teachers, Students, Peers, and Family Members

Support for students' learning seems to expand beyond the UNRWA schools. The 72 UNRWA students interviewed noted that, in addition to their relationships with teachers, principals, and counselors, home and peers were important sources of support for their learning outcomes (figure 3.4).

These multiple sources of support aligned well to theories of child development within different levels in society (or ecologies)[2] and have important implications for supporting community–school partnerships. Alongside teachers, families and peers play a key role in the well-being and education process for at-risk children. Interviewed UNRWA students provided many examples of how parents, siblings, and peers reinforced their learning through additional opportunities to seek information, knowledge, and clarity on a particular topic; by encouraging mutual support and even competition among peers; and by ensuring

Figure 3.4 Different Sources of Support on Learning Outcomes as Perceived by UNRWA Students (Noting the Number of Times It Was Mentioned in Student Interviews)

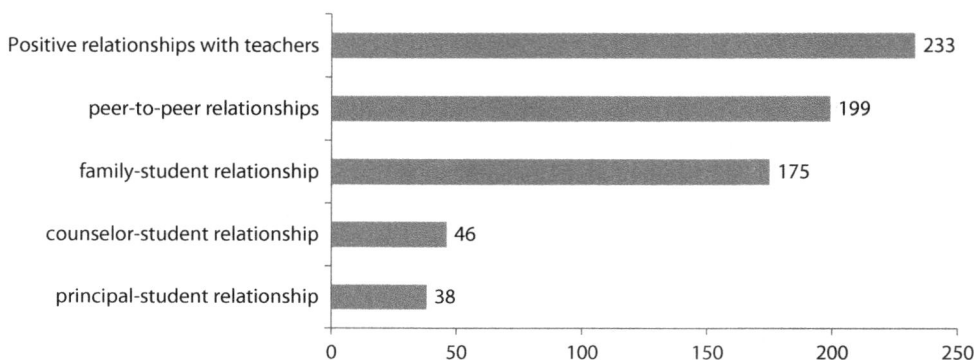

Source: Calculations based on student interviews 2012.

the most viable learning environment possible, or simply providing motivation and encouragement. In the students' own words:

Interviewer: How is your father creating the suitable environment [for your studies]?

Student: He focuses on ensuring the house is quiet, that there is no noise, and I sit in one of the corners of the house and study.

Male student, Gaza

My uncle encourages me when he talks to me, and always tells me stories about college, that some students have educated parents but are not that smart, while there are other students whose parents are not educated but they are very smart. Also, my aunt is a doctor and lives in London, and she always encourages me to become a journalist and to go visit her.

Female student, Gaza

Perhaps the most illustrative example of support for learning is the one among students themselves. For example, UNRWA schools in Gaza tapped into this additional source of learning support by formalizing peer learning techniques in the classroom. The benefits of this are explained by one student:

Interviewer: What do you think of the academic support programs that your school has been holding?

Student: They are so useful and beneficial to weaker students who can ask high performers to help them understand hard materials or test them with some questions. That saves embarrassment from asking this of a teacher. You know that girls feel relaxed when dealing with each other. … We gather with high achievers to read and study and ask about the things that are hard to understand and the high achievers help us in that. If we all don't understand something, we ask our teacher to help us. Sometimes we conduct workshops in the school breaks to discuss issues related to Arabic, math, or science or we broadcast some programs on the useful ways of reading, studying, and obtaining marks. We may print all that and distribute it among the students.

Female student, Gaza

By incorporating strategies to bring schools, families, and peers together, education policies and programs are more likely to be relevant for both quality of learning and protecting students from the adversities they face. Community–school partnerships within the UNRWA system may not be fully structured through formal "school participatory management" models, but they remain organically embedded in the mutual support mechanisms among Palestine refugees. The importance of community–school partnerships for learning outcomes in contexts of adversity merits further study.

UNRWA's Close Partnership with the Refugee Community Creates Shared Accountability for Learning Outcomes

The participation of many stakeholders in supporting the learning process has created a strong matrix of accountability for learning outcomes that stretches across the classroom, school, household, and community of Palestinian refugees. Although students benefit from high expectations placed on them by teachers, head teachers, and parents, students also have high expectations and a clear vision of what the school, their families, and the community can provide. Several students were able to articulate this, as in the following:

> Our community is interested in and appreciates learning. The school ensures the students like going there and enjoy the learning that happens. The goal of the school is to create well-educated students. My family also has a big role in learning, and they will be happy when I finish my learning and graduate from the university with high grades.

> Female student, Gaza

> *Interviewer:* What helps you get high grades?

> *Student:* First, my determination and will; second, the help of my teachers; third, the encouragement of my family. They suffered a lot because their learning stopped and this incentivizes and encourages me to achieve the dreams of my father and my mother. There is also religion that helps us to learn.

> Female student, Gaza

This wider network of support for quality learning in the face of adversity is accountable to each other. Parents checked in on students or were contacted by the school in cases where there was concern about a student's behavior or performance. When students were experiencing problems keeping up with their studies, teachers informed their families and requested help at home. One boy in Gaza explains this:

> My father [not only] used to ask me about my study; he also used to come ask about me at school. Teachers used to tell him that I wasn't doing well, which made him shed light on my studying at home and I started to improve.

Another boy from the West Bank recounted:

> Yes, they know about every grade I get at school, and my father sometimes calls the teachers to ask about my grades, and when I get home he would ask me and tell me not to lie because he knows exactly how much I get. Also my mother comes to school every two weeks to ask about my grades; they do the same for all of us.

Thus, the high expectations and high value placed on learning was strengthened by a shared and mutual school–community accountability to support the learning and well-being of students in a difficult living situation.

What Is Resilience in the UNRWA Education System?

People who exhibit resilience engage in a dynamic process whereby they are able to "navigate" and "negotiate" adversities with the support of relevant opportunities and services.[3] Education resilience—or positive education that results in the face of adversity—is therefore a process and not necessarily a fixed outcome. Results can fluctuate, especially in fast-changing contexts. However, the resilience process can inform how to navigate and negotiate difficult situations. This study points to five education resilience supportive mechanisms identified in UNRWA schools: (1) Students make sense of adversity and find purpose in education, (2) school staff understand the challenges students face and model well-being and a positive identity, (3) student competence in the face of adversity is sustained through academic guidance and socioemotional support, (4) partnerships are fostered across schools, families, and communities, and (5) accountability for learning and protection of students is shared and mutual.

These education resilience strategies at the school and community level are not intended to justify leaving at-risk education communities unaided; rather they are identified as areas that need to be supported by education systems. Interviewed UNRWA students mentioned some of the ways schools and the education system can support their education resilience process. They pointed to seven types of school activities, including general interpersonal relationships, teaching and learning practices, school management, material and financial resources, and assessment, accountability, and discipline.

It can be inferred from the comments of interviewed students that an education resilience perspective appears to be embodied in several of UNRWA's approaches. The UNRWA system triggers resilience-fostering opportunities by a collective sense making of adversity and a holistic vision of education as a meaningful purpose for Palestine refugees. All actors are accountable to this aim and to each other. In practice, UNRWA has been able to tap into a high cultural premium for learning and enhance it with the support of students, parents, teachers, head teachers, and other education staff. The agency has played an important role in fostering positive attitudes toward education and subsequently embracing and enhancing them for the benefit of the wider refugee community through a reinforced network of support for students.

For the students, their refugee status or the daily adversity they face has not made their education dreams less realistic or likely. Instead, these difficulties have made their education more relevant because the system itself is focused on addressing them. UNRWA explicitly articulates its vision of education as a service that balances the specific needs of the population it serves, aligned approaches to the contexts within which they live, and the need for compatibility and competitiveness within the global education priorities. Indeed, UNRWA states that its vision for education is in accordance with the broader UN vision, and it therefore situates its educational developments and priorities within the global frameworks of the Millennium Development Goals and the Education for All initiative (UNRWA 2013). Yet, it also provides its own agency-level interpretation of this, which translates to the skills and competencies it would like to transmit to its students. According to the agency's Commissioner General: "The fundamental goal of UNRWA's Education programme is to ensure that the children who come out of our schools know how to think in a critical, independent, intelligent manner. And to do this, we need to review the manner in which they learn" (UNRWA n.d., 1).

One commentator suggests that UNRWA seeks to meet this challenge by implementing locally defined curriculum content within a model of "western, secular, liberal education" (Bocco 2010, 245), based on a specific and articulated UN vision for education to achieve sustainable positive impact in the face of adversity. The resilience data collected for this study complement this and suggest that a strong commitment at the systems level and varied accessible forms of support for its students support the attainment of positive learning outcomes in the midst of a difficult context. This is what Maya Rosenfeld's historical perspective alludes to the following: "the consolidation of UNRWA as an education-centered agency facilitated a transformation in the educational and occupational profiles of second- and third-generation refugees of both genders. … UNRWA's pioneering efforts to universalize a basic education of nine years and to promote the attainment of secondary and professional education enabled young Palestinian refugees to achieve an 'educational advantage' over their peers in the Arab host countries" (Rosenfeld 2010).[4]

Specifically, for the Palestine refugees who participated in this study, learning in adversity is about much more than a simple classroom dynamic, but rather comprises an active engagement of the whole community around education, and the commitment and vision of the service provider to provide them with locally relevant and accessible opportunities through which to fulfill their potential and, crucially, to make transformative contributions to their communities. In the words of UNRWA Commissioner General, Filippo Grandi, speaking at the 30th Anniversary Conference of the Refugee Studies Centre, Oxford University, December 7, 2012:

> UNRWA's work, in spite of multiple challenges, was made easier by the exceptional resilience and resourcefulness of the Palestinians. Their accomplishments have become part of the folklore instilled in each succeeding generation of refugees. They reveal the depth of the refugee will—the universal will of refugees, if I may say so—to self-improvement, to shape their lives against overwhelming odds, and to contribute positively to the dynamic of development in their communities, in the societies hosting them, and the world at large.
>
> UNRWA, and the international community that sustains it, share credit in the continuing contribution to the human capital of the refugees. It is, however, the refugees that have seized opportunities and made their own way into the firmament of business, skilled professions, civil society, and public service, in every continent around the globe. In exercising social mobility despite the many

handicaps against them, Palestine refugees—just like so many other refugees with whom I have had the privilege to work in my professional life—call our attention to their ambitions, resourcefulness, and creativity.

UNRWA's experience in providing education is an important one to help us better understand what education resilience means at the systems level. Resilience research takes as its starting point a context of risk or adversity. From this, however, assets—strengths, opportunities, and capacities—already existing within the system are identified. Resilience-relevant interventions can then build on these assets to provide vulnerable students with more mechanisms and opportunities to "navigate" and "negotiate"[5] the risks they face. They are not left alone. This chapter considered this process relative to the UNRWA system and was indeed able to identify important supportive processes embedded within the system. These lessons could support UNRWA to adopt a more explicit resilience approach to its work and may also provide useful lessons for other education systems in similar contexts. To conclude, figure 3.5 provides a schematic overview of the education resilience lessons learned by the insightful comments of 72 UNRWA students who themselves exemplify *learning in the face of adversity.*

Relevance of Findings

The United Nations Relief and Works Agency (UNRWA) has delivered quality education, significantly outperforming two public school systems, under challenging circumstances. Such resilience does not imply that UNRWA is immune

Figure 3.5   The Five Education Resilience Supportive Mechanisms Identified in UNRWA Schools

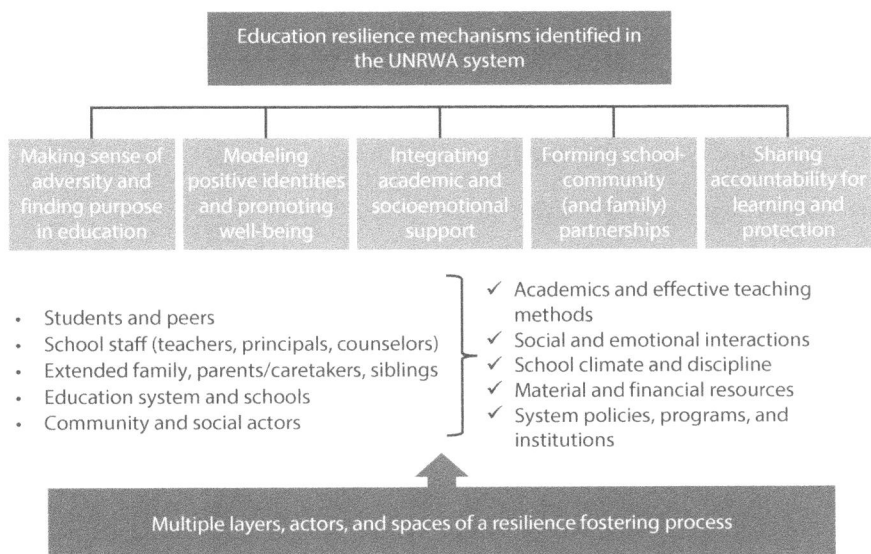

Education resilience mechanisms identified in the UNRWA system

| Making sense of adversity and finding purpose in education | Modeling positive identities and promoting well-being | Integrating academic and socioemotional support | Forming school-community (and family) partnerships | Sharing accountability for learning and protection |

- Students and peers
- School staff (teachers, principals, counselors)
- Extended family, parents/caretakers, siblings
- Education system and schools
- Community and social actors

✓ Academics and effective teaching methods
✓ Social and emotional interactions
✓ School climate and discipline
✓ Material and financial resources
✓ System policies, programs, and institutions

Multiple layers, actors, and spaces of a resilience fostering process

to crisis. Indeed, since 2007, several significant events have complicated the service delivery climate in the West Bank and Gaza and Jordan. These include the blockade on Gaza that began in 2006, economic sanctions, withholding of tax revenues, ongoing military and militant operations, Palestinian internal politics, and the events of the Arab Spring. Although exogenous to the education system, these factors are likely to have had—and continue to have—an impact on both refugees and nonrefugee education systems, and they may help account for the overall general decrease in learning outcomes.[6]

Moreover, UNRWA's sustained competitiveness in such adverse contexts (occupation, armed conflict, restricted movement, and protracted displacement) still presents important lessons for other school systems. Specifically, the effective classroom practices of teachers, strong school leadership, assessments, and shared accountability for learning are strong features in the UNRWA system that can support organizational adaptability and performance in the face of adversity. Equally important is recognizing the risks and vulnerabilities that students face and fostering relevant interactions across school and community actors to support learning and protection of students in such challenging contexts. A resilience approach does not imply that schools and communities at risk are left to fend for themselves, but calls for an alignment and institutionalization of education systems to support the resilience processes of which students, teachers, and families avail themselves. As such, the UNRWA experience merits further exploration and investigation to sustain in a difficult context the quality learning opportunities for all children and youth. Figure 3.6 shows some identified ways in which schools could support the resilience process.

Figure 3.6   The Different Ways in Which Schools Support the Resilience Process (Noting the Number of Times It Was Mentioned in Student Interviews)

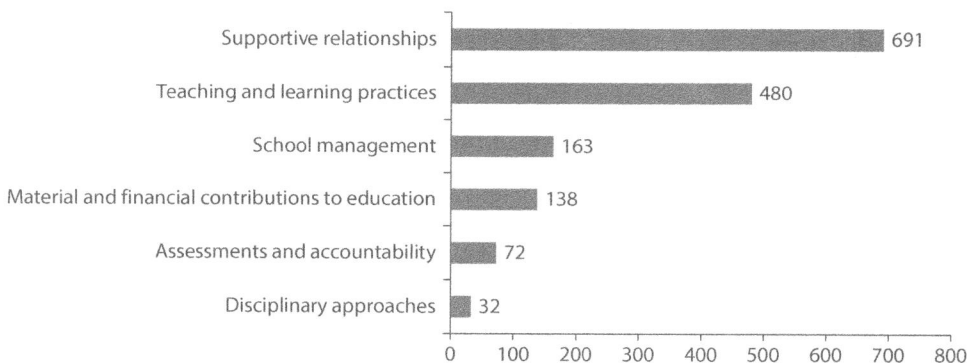

Source: Calculations based on student interviews, 2012.

Notes

1. UNRWA lacks legislative or authoritative power, and so implementing such values must be done at the classroom level, through the teaching staff. Given the importance of this approach for students, additional studies that explore UNRWA's teacher training and professional development programs and associated incentives could reveal important findings.

2. Of note is Bronfenbrenner (1974).

3. For more on the resilience process, see Ungar (2012) and Liebenberg and Ungar (2008).

4. Data collected for this study are contrary to Rosenfeld's claim in this article that the UNRWA "educational advantage" persisted until the 1980s but has since not been reproduced. Yet, this does not negate her central argument that adverse conditions and development in the region may have resulted in decreases in declining student performance in the recent past.

5. Using the terminology of Ungar (2008) and (2011).

6. A recent World Bank report (2013a, 2) concluded that the prevailing situation was resulting in lasting damage and that "much bolder efforts to create the basis for a viable economy need to be made to prevent the continued deterioration that will have lasting and costly implications for economic competiveness and social cohesion." See also World Bank (2013b).

Methodology

SABER

Systems Approach for Better Education Results (SABER)-Teachers and SABER-School Autonomy were implemented systematically. Information on a set of questions was obtained and then aggregated into preestablished indicators—and corresponding subindicators—to assess outcome in each policy area. The strength of the indicators is tied to the depth and scope of the programs and policies associated with it. The degree of indicator strength reflects what is implemented on the ground. At the low level of indicator strength, the policy is not implemented, whereas at the high level there is complete implementation of the policy. Following are SABER-Teachers' 10 core policy areas:

- Requirements to enter and remain in teaching
- Initial teacher preparation
- Recruitment and employment
- Teachers' workload and autonomy
- Professional development
- Compensation (salary and nonsalary benefits)
- Retirement rules and benefits
- Monitoring and evaluation of teacher quality
- Teacher representation and voice
- School leadership.

SABER–School Autonomy and Accountability has identified five core policy goals that are important in assessing school-based management policies:

- School autonomy in the planning and management of the school budget
- School autonomy in personnel management
- Role of the school council in school governance
- School and student assessment
- Accountability to stakeholders.

Stallings Classroom Observation

The Stallings observation system[1] consists of three main instruments: (1) the Physical Environment Information, (2) the Classroom Snapshot, and (3) the Five-Minute Interaction. Only the Classroom Snapshot was used for this study.

The *Classroom Snapshot* records all the participants in the classroom, what they are doing, and with whom they are engaged (Stallings 1977). It is completed by a classroom observer and recorded in a grid that includes all adults in the classroom (teacher, teacher aide, and visitor), all possible combinations of students (one, two, small groups, and large groups), and 15 categories of activities (such as arts/crafts, tables/games/and so on, math, reading, social studies, science, dramatic play, practical skills, social interaction, discipline, transitional activities, classroom management, and so on). There are a total of 22 rows of such activities in the snapshot, and the observer marks what the adults are doing and the corresponding arrangement of students. Stallings (1983) reports that the snapshot form looks formidable, but that it is rather efficient and easy to use, with teachers and administrators learning to use it satisfactorily in just two half-day training sessions.

The tool was implemented in a stratified sample (based on Trends in International Mathematics and Science Study [TIMSS] 2007 school performance, type, location, and size) of 50 United Nations Relief and Works Agency (UNRWA) schools and 50 public control schools and was selected following the 2007 TIMSS sampling framework. The stratification is based on school location in terms of population concentration and proximity to other schools as a proxy for competition.

Implementation was carried out in each school in the sample by a six-person team of observers three times in the winter term of the 2011–12 school year. Observers were unaware of the classification of school to be visited. An eighth grade class was also visited, and observers collected data using the snapshot and five-minute interaction tools. At the end of the observations, UNRWA schools were compared with public schools using the different domains of the instruments. To carry out this process, a research team was recruited and trained to conduct the field work. A regional supervisor followed up on implementation and worked with coordinators in each of the three fields. In each selected school, three classes (math class, science class and reading class) were visited three times during the fall session (September to December 2011) by two observers. The same observers who visited the UNRWA schools also visited the public schools in each field of operation. The fieldwork was managed and coordinated by an international consultant based in Washington, DC, and a regional coordinator supervised the data collection in Jordan and coordinated with two supervisors: one in the West Bank and one in Gaza. Each member of the research team received a structured training to familiarize them with the research methodology and use of the Stallings instruments.

This process was carried out by two international experts with prior training experience. Six researchers and a field supervisor were recruited from each of the regions to conduct the classroom observations. All 18 field researchers were retired school teachers. Training and certification workshops were conducted for each of the three regions. Three local researchers with doctorate degrees and extensive field experience supervised the field work (and were trained and certified on the Stallings tool, as well).

In each school selected in the sample, three eighth-grade classes were selected to be observed covering Arabic language, mathematics, and science subjects. Each school visit also included a school instrument to be filled out by the researcher with information from the school principal before the observation. The observers filled out a class inventory survey before the beginning of the snapshots. Then, from each class, they filled out 10 snapshots. After the training, the team piloted the instruments in four schools in West Bank, four schools in Gaza, and three schools in Jordan. Data were collected during the month of November 2011. In the end, 1,800 snapshots were collected.

All data were sent to a central location in Jordan, and data specialists entered the data using WinDEM[2] software. In addition to the coded field checking, each snapshot was entered twice for data confirmation before finalizing the entry. Finally, all data were converted to STATA for analysis.

To compare with other countries in which the snapshot was implemented, activities were grouped into: learning activities, classroom management, and teacher off-task. Table A.1 shows the classification of activities into these categories.

Qualitative Data Approach

The UNRWA resilience component was undertaken using qualitative data collection and analysis methods. Seventy-two high-performing UNRWA students of refugee families in most difficult situations in and outside camps were interviewed in three of UNRWA's fields of operations: the West Bank and Gaza and Jordan. This was a purposeful sample of eighth and ninth graders who were selected according to predetermined resilience criteria: (1) They had higher-than-average school grades, and (2) they came from families which received additional school and social services due to difficult life situations. All students remained anonymous and provided their assent to be interviewed along adult

Table A.1 Teacher Time Categorization

a. Learning activities	Reading aloud, demonstration/lecture, discussion, practice and drill, assignment/classwork, copying
b. Classroom management	Verbal instruction, discipline, classroom management, classroom management alone
c. Teacher off-task	Teacher social interaction or teacher uninvolved, teacher out of the room
d. Student off-task	Social interaction, student(s) uninvolved, discipline

consent. To understand the context of adversity that affects all Palestinian youth, 24 additional interviews with similar youth in public schools in the three fields were also conducted. This complementary sample of interviews from outside the UNRWA system helped us better understand the contexts of adversity of Palestinian youth in general. All students were interviewed in Arabic by local researchers for half an hour during which time they were asked about the challenges they had faced and how they had performed academically in spite of this (see box A.1).

All interviews followed a similar format: Children were questioned about the challenges they faced and the support mechanisms that they utilized in the home, community, and school environment. In addition to talking about their individual approaches to pursuing education success, the Palestinian students also shed light on those environmental factors that promote learning despite adversity (in other words, they identified sources of support for the resilience process). Their understanding and reasoning regarding the risks and obstacles they encounter, as well as their stated educational goals and purpose, were an important starting point from which to subsequently identify which aspects of the school system propel them toward resilience.

Following completion of the data collection, the interviews were entered into NVivo, which is qualitative data analysis software. NVivo was chosen owing to its appropriateness for qualitative data collection and the ability to use it to support the construction of a grounded theory of the education resilience mechanisms in the UNRWA system. Given the open-ended interview questions, there was significant complexity in the coding (from general open coding, to more focused categories, to axial relations within and between categories identified). NVivo allowed for greater ease in the identification of themes and patterns within and between codes and supported us to adhere to a rigorous process through which theories and concepts could emerge and be interpreted from the qualitative data set available. This was especially important, given that the study was neither of a representative nor statistically significant sample of students, but rather of a purposefully selected group of students with the lived experiences that could yield light on the topic of interest: learning in a context of adversity.

Box A.1 Interviewee Demographic Data

- Fifty-three percent of those interviewed were male and 47 percent female.
- All students were aged 13–16 years and were studying in grades 8–10.
- Each field was attributed a third of the total interviews.
- Ten different neighborhoods were included in the study: three in Gaza, three in Jordan, and four in the West Bank.
- Forty-four percent of the interviewees lived in refugee camps, and 52 percent lived outside of camp settings.

Once the data were uploaded into the software, we began a process of coding references made within each and every one of the interviews in accordance with the following broad categories:

- Types of adversity
- Meaning of education
- Emerging thematic dimensions
- Sources of support.

Within these categories, many more subcategories were identified. Thus, "types of adversity" was subcategorized into adversity present in different spheres of the students' social context (home, school, community, or stemming from the conflict). "Meaning of education" was attributed from the purpose that students accorded to their studies: self-improvement, financial motivation, family support, community betterment, or national goals. Similarly, "sources of support" were broken down based on their genesis (from members of the family, from the students themselves, from different actors within the education system, or from the peer group). These three levels of analysis resulted in more than 130 different codes. Some segments of the text were coded with multiple codes.

The key themes as they relate to both adversity and sources of support provided an important foundation upon which to conduct our subsequent analysis. Once these have been presented, we will then consider how those supportive school-level approaches[3]—be they implicitly or explicitly mentioned in the narratives of the youth—address the adversities identified and relate to resilience theory and literature. At this stage, theoretical elements and key findings within the resilience literature helped us interpret the students' narratives in a more integrated way. We also sought to make use of the study's mixed methods approach to bring together and even note the differences across our findings from the different data collection tools. As Bazeley (2002, 9) posits, "In determining how best to present the ideas and evidence generated through the completed study, the issue becomes one of the degree to which quantitative and qualitative components can or should be integrated."

In this way, our analysis for the 72 UNRWA students follows a three-tier, or leveled, process:

1. The codification of themes regarding adversities experienced (this included 24 additional interviews with public system students), the related purpose or reason for education success, and the sources for support for learning in spite of adversity.
2. The qualitative analysis led us to five key education resilience mechanisms: making sense and finding purpose, seeking identity and well-being; having competence and control through academic and socioemotional support; connecting with others; and committing and being accountable. For presentation purposes, narrative segments were selected to substantiate these five mechanisms.

3. Grounded on the UNRWA students' stories of education resilience, we develop a theory or hypothesis of the possible relationship between education system support and academic outcomes in spite of adversity.

Methodological Limitations

Our choice of mixed methods was intended to allow for a more comprehensive evidence base that captures the process aspects of resilience mechanisms. Nevertheless, it is important here to state the limitations that our chosen data collection tools present. In other words, what inferences are we able to make from the evidence base and what are we not?

With regard to the classroom observations, although subjectivity was highlighted in training and certification sessions of the researchers before the beginning of the task, the classroom observers and interviewers were likely to know if the school was an UNRWA school or a public school.

With regard to the qualitative data, the sample size used for interviews is always small, allowing the researcher to probe deeper into complex relationships and new information. Thus, this type of "small n" cannot be held as representative for all UNRWA schools or the three fields of operation. Rather, qualitative data seek to identify important characteristics to facilitate both exploration and explanation of the research questions. Theoretical analysis and conceptualization of the new topics identified in the students' narratives allow us to make inferences regarding the processes and mechanisms that support education resilience—learning in a context of adversity—in addition to those preidentified by the quantitative measures. The sample of students in public schools is not meant to be representative of the public system, nor "a control group" for the UNRWA resilience findings. This much smaller sample of public schools was selected and is intended not as a point of comparison but rather as a check against which to compare the context of adversity across Palestinian youth—inside and outside of the UNRWA system. There was a strong convergence between UNRWA and non-UNRWA students on their reports of the proximal and external risks experienced by Palestinian youth in the West Bank and Gaza and Jordan. In this way, the bulk of the analysis for the education resilience component centers on the data collected from UNRWA schools alone. Finally, and to reiterate, we are not looking to establish whether the students in our sample are "resilient" but rather what process mechanisms and inputs help them in their resilience.

Notes

1. Several classroom observations exist. For more on the history of classroom observation, see Lewin, Lippitt, and White (1939), Anderson and Brewer (1945), Thelen (1951), Flanders (1962), Withall and Lewis (1963), Simon and Boyer (1967–70), Medley (1982), Stallings (1977), and Stallings and Mohlman (1990). Stallings and Mohlman (1990) addressed the delineation of common elements across all "observational techniques." These common elements include (a) purpose, (b) a set of operational

definitions, (c) a means to train observers, (d) a focus on observation, (e) a setting, (f) a unit of time, (g) an observation schedule (timing of data collection, not the observation form itself), (h) a method to record data, and (i) a method to process and analyze data.

2. Open source data entry tool by International Association for the Evaluation of Educational Achievement data processing center.

3. Here, we will draw upon school effectiveness theory to better structure and subsequently analyze school-based approaches.

References

Abadzi, H. 2009. "Instructional Time Loss in Developing Countries: Concepts, Measurement, and Implications." *World Bank Research Observer* 24 (2): 267–90.

Anderson, H. H., and H. M. Brewer. 1945. *Studies of Teachers' Classroom Personalities. I. Dominative and Socially Integrative Behavior of Kindergarten Teachers.* Applied Psychology Monographs 6. Stanford: Stanford University Press.

Banerjee, A. V., R. Banerji, E. Duflo, R. Glennerster, and S. Khemani. 2010. "Pitfalls of Participatory Programs: Evidence from a Randomized Evaluation in Education in India." *American Economic Journal: Economic Policy* 2 (1): 1–30.

Barrera-Osorio, F., T. Fasih, and H. A. Patrinos. 2009. *Decentralized Decision-Making in Schools: The Theory and Evidence on School-Based Management.* Washington, DC: World Bank.

Bazeley, P. 2002. "Issues in Mixing Qualitative and Quantitative Approaches to Research." *AIDS* 21 (2): S91–S98.

Blinder, A. 1973. "Wage Discrimination: Reduced Form and Structural Estimates." *Journal of Human Resources* 8 (4): 436–55.

Bocco, R. 2010. "UNRWA and the Palestinian Refugees: A History within History." *Refugee Survey Quarterly* 28 (2–3): 229–52.

Bronfenbrenner, Urie. 1974. "Developmental Research, Public Policy, and the Ecology of Childhood." *Child Development* 45: 1–5.

Bruns, B., D. Filmer, and H. A. Patrinos. 2011. *Making Schools Work: New Evidence on Accountability Reforms.* Washington, DC: World Bank.

Filmer, D., and L. Pritchett. 1998. "Estimating Wealth Effects without Expenditure Data—Or Tears: With an Application to Educational Enrollments in States of India." World Bank Policy Research Working Paper 1994, Development Economics Research Group, World Bank, Washington, DC.

Flanders, N. A. 1962. "Using Interaction Analysis in the In-service Training of Teachers." *Journal of Experimental Education* 30 (4): 313–16.

Grandi, Filippo. n.d. "UNRWA Education: Learning Together." http://www.unrwa.org/sites/default/files/2012080244052.pdf.

Lewin, K., R. Lippitt, and R. K. White. 1939. "Patterns of Aggressive Behavior in Experimentally Created Social Climates." *Journal of Social Psychology* 10: 271–301.

Liebenberg, L., and M. Ungar, eds. 2008. *Resilience in Action.* Toronto: University of Toronto Press.

Medley, D. M. 1982. "Systemic Observation." In *Encyclopedia of Educational Research*, 5th ed., edited by H. E. Mitzel, J. H. Best, and W. Rabinowitz, 1841–51. New York: Free Press.

Oaxaca, R. 1973. "Male-Female Wages Differentials in Urban Labor Markets." *International Economic Review* 14 (3): 693–709.

Rosenfeld, M. 2010. "From Emergency Relief Assistance to Human Development and Back: UNRWA and the Palestinian Refugees, 1950–2009." *Refugee Survey Quarterly* 28 (2–3): 286–317.

Simon, A., and E. G. Boyer, eds. 1967–70. *Mirrors for Behavior: An Anthology of Classroom Observation Instruments*. 14 vols. Philadelphia: Research for Better Schools.

Stallings, J. A. 1977. *Learning to Look: A Handbook on Classroom Observation and Teaching Models*. Belmont, CA: Wadsworth Publishing.

———. 1983. "The Stallings Observation System." Unpublished manuscript, George Peabody College, Vanderbilt University, Nashville.

Stallings, J. A., and G. G. Mohlman. 1990. "Issues in Qualitative Evaluation Research: Observation Techniques." In *The International Encyclopedia of Educational Evaluation*, edited by H. J. Walberg and G. D. Haertel, 639–44. New York: Pergamon Press.

Thelen, H. 1951. "Experimental Research toward a Theory of Instruction." *Journal of Educational Research* 45 (2): 89–93.

Ungar, M. 2008. "Resilience across Cultures." *British Journal of Social Work* 38 (2): 218–35.

———. 2011. "Community Resilience for Youth and Families: Facilitative Physical and Social Capital in Contexts of Adversity." *Children and Youth Social Services Review* 33: 1742–48.

———, ed. 2012. *The Social Ecology of Resilience: A Handbook*. New York: Springer.

UNRWA. 2008. "What Protection Means for UNRWA in Concept and Practice." http://www.unrwa.org/userfiles/20100118155412.pdf.

———. 2013. "UNRWA Programme Budget for 2012–2013." http://www.unrwa.org/userfiles/file/financial_updates/2011/Blue%20Book%202012-2013.pdf.

———. n.d. "Education Learning Together." http://www.unrwa.org/user-files/2012112174018.pdf.

Withall, J., and W. W. Lewis. 1963. "Social Interaction in the Classroom." In *Handbook of Research on Teaching*, edited by. N. L. Gage. Chicago: Rand McNally.

World Bank. 2011. "SABER School Autonomy & Accountability." Human Development Network/Education, World Bank, Washington, DC. http://saber.worldbank.org/index.cfm?indx=8&tb=4.

———. 2012. "SABER Teachers." Human Development Network/Education, World Bank, Washington, DC. http://saber.worldbank.org/index.cfm?indx=8&tb=1.

———. 2013a. "Fiscal Challenges and Long Term Economic Costs. Economic Monitoring Report to the Ad Hoc Liaison Committee." World Bank, Washington, DC.

———. 2013b. "Palestinian Economy Is Losing Long-Term Competitiveness." Press release, March 11. World Bank, Washington, DC. http://www.worldbank.org/en/news/press-release/2013/03/11/palestinian-economy-losing-long-term-competitiveness.

———. 2013c. "The What, Why, and How of the Systems Approach for Better Education Results (SABER) (Conference Edition)." World Bank, Washington, DC.

ECO-AUDIT

Environmental Benefits Statement

The World Bank Group is committed to reducing its environmental footprint. In support of this commitment, the Publishing and Knowledge Division leverages electronic publishing options and print-on-demand technology, which is located in regional hubs worldwide. Together, these initiatives enable print runs to be lowered and shipping distances decreased, resulting in reduced paper consumption, chemical use, greenhouse gas emissions, and waste.

The Publishing and Knowledge Division follows the recommended standards for paper use set by the Green Press Initiative. The majority of our books are printed on Forest Stewardship Council (FSC)–certified paper, with nearly all containing 50–100 percent recycled content. The recycled fiber in our book paper is either unbleached or bleached using totally chlorine free (TCF), processed chlorine free (PCF), or enhanced elemental chlorine free (EECF) processes.

More information about the Bank's environmental philosophy can be found at http://crinfo.worldbank.org/wbcrinfo/node/4.

green
press
INITIATIVE

www.ingramcontent.com/pod-product-compliance
Lightning Source LLC
Chambersburg PA
CBHW080002280326
41935CB00013B/1722